LOG IN TO ENGLISH 1

Editora: Ana Rita de S. Corrêa

CB131719

Richmond

Scope & Sequence

		FUNCTION	GRAMMAR	LEXIS	RECYCLING
WELCOME					
L1	p.4	Introducing oneself: Greeting and saying goodbye.	Verb *to be* (*am, is, are*)	The alphabet; Greetings; Numbers 1 – 20	
L2	p.6	Asking each other's names & age.	Verb *to be* (*am, is, are*)	Spelling; School objects & classroom commands	
UNIT 1		Talking about myself			
L1	p.8	Asking & giving personal information. Asking & saying where one is from.	Question words: *what, where & how old* Preposition: *from* Possessive adjectives: *my & your*	Countries & nationalities	What's your (last) name? How old are you? I'm nineteen (years old)
L2	p.10	Asking information about other people.	Verb *to be* (aff.) Subject pronouns: *I, you, he, she* Where + *to be*	Countries & nationalities	Countries & nationalities *Where are you from?*
L3	p.12	Describing flags from different countries. Asking where one is from & what color something is.	Verb *to be* (int.) & short answers Subject pronoun: it	Colors	Verb *to be* (aff.) Subject pronouns: *I, you, he & she* Countries & Nationalities
L4	p.14	Asking & saying when one's birthday is & one's e-mail address and phone number.	Question words: *when & how* Preposition *in* + month	Months of the year	Question word: *what*
Review Lesson Unit 1 **(p.16)**			World Issues Magazine - WI1: *We are all in this world together!*		
UNIT 2		Talking about myself & others			
L1	p.18	Describing people.	Verb *to be* (neg.) Subject pronouns: *we & they*	Parts of the body Adjectives (physical characteristics & personality)	Verb *to be* (aff. & neg.) Colors e-mail
L2	p.20	Talking about one's favorite movie star, athlete. Giving opinion.	Verb *to be* & short answers	Occupations Sports	Verb *to be* (aff., neg. & int.) + short answers Describing people
L3	p.22	Talking about people's favorite characters & describing them.	Possessive adjectives: *my, his & her.*	Adjectives	Parts of the body Describing people
L4	p.24	Saying whether an adjective has a positive or a negative connotation. Giving opinion about people.	Possessive adjectives: *our & their*	Opinion adjectives Titles (*Mr., Miss, Mrs., Ms.*)	Possessive adjectives: *my, your, his & her*
Review Lesson Unit 2 **(p.26)**			World Issues Magazine - WI2: *What's beauty?*		
UNIT 3		My things			
L1	p.28	Asking what something is & how one says something in English.	Demonstrative pronouns: *this & that* Indefinite articles: *a & an*	School objects	*It's...*
L2	p.30	Asking what things are & saying whose things are. Asking how one says some words in English.	Demonstrative pronouns: *these & those* Possessive *'s*	Personal objects	*They are...*
L3	p.32	Making suggestions. Accepting / not accepting the suggestions.	*Let's* + verb	Objects	Verb *to be* (all forms) *This, that, these & those* Possessive *'s*
L4	p.34	Connecting ideas using *and* or *but.*	Conjunctions: *and & but*		Verb *to be* (all forms) Adjectives Physical description
Review Lesson Unit 3 **(p.36)**			World Issues Magazine - WI3: *Friends around the world*		
UNIT 4		My school & neighborhood			
L1	p.38	Describing one's school.	*There is / There are* (aff.)	School & neighborhood facilities	Sports Indefinite articles Prepositions of place
L2	p.40	Asking & saying where things are.	*Where is / are...?* Prepositions of place	Objects	Verb *to be* (all forms) *It's... / They're...* There's / there are...
L3	p.42	Asking & giving information about one's neighborhood.	*There is / There are* (aff., neg. & int.) + short answers *Any & no*	Neighborhood facilities	Giving opinion Prepositions of place There is (aff.)
L4	p.44	Asking about quantities.	Question word: *how many...* Pronoun: *none*	Numbers: 20 – 50	There is / there are School facilities Prepositions of place
Review Lesson Unit 4 **(p.46)**			World Issues Magazine - WI4: *The place where we live*		

Welcome Unit

Lesson 1

READING & LISTENING

1 **Read the school bulletin board. Listen and repeat.** 2

PRACTICE

2 **Check (✓) the correct questions. Listen and repeat.** 3

1. ◯ What's your name?
   ◯ How old are you?
   Jeremy.
2. ◯ What about you?
   ◯ What's your last name?
   Graham.
3. ◯ How do you spell it?
   ◯ How are you?
   G-R-A-H-A-M.
4. ◯ What's your name?
   ◯ How old are you?
   I'm 12.

Tip 4
The alphabet
Listen and repeat.

3 **Imagine Sarah Dean is answering the questions in #2 now. Write her answers.**

1 ______________________
2 ______________________
3 ______________________
4 ______________________

4 **Now tell us about YOU. Answer the questions.**

1 What's your name? ______________________
2 What's your last name? ______________________
3 How do you spell it? ______________________
4 How old are you? ______________________
5 What class are you in? ______________________

Vocabulary Box

Numbers

1 one	11 eleven
2 two	12 twelve
3 three	13 thirteen
4 four	14 fourteen
5 five	15 fifteen
6 six	16 sixteen
7 seven	17 seventeen
8 eight	18 eighteen
9 nine	19 nineteen
10 ten	20 twenty

READING & LISTENING

5 **Rita and Sarah meet for the first time at Green Valley School. Read and number the dialogue in order. Listen and check.**

5

( ) Dean? How do you spell it?
(7) I'm 12. What about you?
( ) I'm in class 5B too. That's great! Have to go! Goodbye, Sarah.
(1) Hi!
(3) I'm Rita. Rita Sanchez. What's your name?

( ) D-E-A-N. How old are you, Rita?
( ) I'm 11. I'm in class 5B.
( ) Bye, Rita. See you!
( ) Hello.
( ) Sarah. Sarah Dean.

LOG IN

6 **Practice with a classmate.**
Have a similar conversation based on #5.

VOCABULARY WORK

school objects

1 **This is a classroom at Green Valley School. Look at the objects and number the words.**

[ ] a clock
[ ] a pencil
[ ] a computer
[ ] a door
[ ] a desk
[ ] a whiteboard
[ ] a notebook
[ ] a pencil case
[ ] a book
[ ] a pen
[ ] an eraser
[ ] a wastebasket

2 **Choose a word from #1 and make a sentence.**

____

____

____

PRACTICE

3 **Cover the words in #1. Play a *spelling game*.**

A Listen: C – O – M – P – U – T – E – R.
B I know! A computer!
Can you repeat that, please?
I don't know.

VOCABULARY WORK

classroom commands

4 **Mr. Brown is a teacher at Green Valley School. Learn some expressions he uses with his students in the classroom.**

1 ◯ Open your book.

2 ◯ Close the door.

3 ◯ Look at the board.

4 ◯ Read the text.

5 ◯ Listen to the CD.

6 ◯ Write your name.

7 ◯ May I go to the bathroom?

8 ◯ Can I get some water, please?

5 **Go back to #4. Check (✓) the sentences YOU hear your teacher say in your classroom.**

6 **Mr. Brown is talking to his students. Complete the dialogue. Use the expressions and words from #4. Listen and check.**

6

Mr. Brown Let's get started. [1] ______________________ to page 7.
[2] ______________________ the CD and [3] ______________________ the text.

Alice Excuse me, Mr. Brown. [4] ______________________ some water, please?

Mr. Brown OK, Alice, but hurry up! Don't forget to
[5] ______________________ the door
when you come back.

Want more?
Go to Word Log - Welcome Lesson (p. 97)

Unit 1

Talking about myself

Lesson 1

READING & LISTENING

1 **Listen and check (✓) the correct options.**

7

Andy Hi, Dianna. I'm Andy from class 7C.

◯ What's your last name?

◯ What's your full name?

Dianna It's Dianna Blair.

Andy ◯ Where are you from?

◯ How old are you?

Dianna I'm from the USA.

Andy ◯ What's your name?

◯ How old are you?

Dianna I'm 18 years old.

COMPREHENSION

2 **Now complete Dianna's profile.**

Book online

22 scraps | 9 photos | 13 fans | 2 videos

profile ▼

Name: ____________________

Age: ______ years old

Country: ____________________

Nationality: American

home

events (25)

friends ▼

135 friends see all

Paul (128)

Lisa (31)

Mariah (287)

LANGUAGE LOGIN

Question words & Personal information

What's your name?	My name's Dianna Blair.
Where are you from?	I'm from the USA. I'm American.
How old are you?	I'm eighteen (years old).

Attention! Use **from** + country

Possessive adjectives: my & your

What's **your** name? → **My** name's Chris.

VOCABULARY WORK

countries & nationalities

3 **Match the countries and the nationalities. Listen to your teacher and repeat.**

	Country		Nationality
1	Argentina	(10)	Japanese
2	Brazil	(11)	South African
3	Canada	(4)	Chinese
4	China	(1)	Argentinian
5	France	(12)	American
6	Germany	(5)	French
7	Great Britain	(3)	Canadian
8	Mexico	(6)	German
9	Italy	(2)	Brazilian
10	Japan	(9)	Italian
11	South Africa	(7)	British
12	the USA	(8)	Mexican

Tip

In English, countries and nationalities begin with CAPITAL LETTERS.

Look: I'm from Mexico.
I'm Mexican.

PRACTICE

4 **Complete.**

LOG IN

5 **Practice with a classmate.**
Start with the model below. Add new questions.

A My name's Barbara Walker. I'm 14. I'm American. Where are you from?
B I'm from Mexico.

RECYCLING

1 **Go to #3 on page 9 and test your friend.**

A Brazilian?
B Brazil. China?
A Chinese...

GO GET IT

to be from + country

2 **John and Paula are talking about famous people they know. Look at the Language Login. Listen, read and complete.**

8

John	Where are you from?
Paula	I'm [1] ______________ Brazil.
John	Where's Ronaldinho Gaúcho from?
Paula	He's from [2] ______________ too!
John	Where's J. K. Rowling from? I don't know.
Paula	I think she's from [3] ______________ .
John	You're so smart!

Lesson 2

READING & COMPREHENSION

3 **Read the sentences. Match them to the correct picture.**

- ◯ This person is a singer. She's very famous. She's Colombian.
- ◯ This person is a singer too. She's from Canada.
- ◯ He's a soccer player. Where's he from? Brazil.
- ◯ He's from Great Britain. He's a famous soccer player.

3

1

2

LANGUAGE LOGIN

Verb to be: aff.

I **am** = I'**m** from Japan.
You **are** = You'**re** French.
He **is** = He'**s** Brazilian.
She **is** = She'**s** South African.

Where **is** = Where'**s** he from? He'**s** from Italy.
Where **is** = Where'**s** she from? She'**s** from China.

Attention! Use **he** for boys & men and **she** for girls & women

GO GET IT

he & she

4 **Look at the Language Login. Complete using *he's* or *she's*.**

1 Gisele Bündchen is from Brazil. ________ Brazilian.
2 Where's Bill Gates from?
I think ________ from the USA.
3 Hugh Jackman is a famous actor. ________ Australian.
4 Penelope Cruz is Spanish. ________ an actress.
5 Where's Cate Blanchett from?
________ from Australia.
6 Lewis Hamilton is a famous Formula 1 driver.
________ British.

4

PRACTICE

5 **Now YOU answer the questions.**
Use: *I think he's / she's* or *I don't know.*

1 Where's Zac Efron from?
____
2 How old is he?
____
3 Where's Reese Witherspoon from?
____
4 How old is she?
____

LOG IN

6 **Practice with a classmate.**
Think of a famous person and ask questions about him or her. Use #5 for help.

VOCABULARY WORK

colors

1 Match the colors and the words.

- ◯ blue
- ◯ orange
- ◯ red
- ◯ black
- ◯ brown
- ◯ pink
- ◯ white
- ◯ green
- ◯ gray
- ◯ purple
- ◯ yellow

PRACTICE

2 Write the correct country.

1 This flag is black, yellow, green, white, blue and red. Where's it from? It's from ______________ .

2 This flag is white and red. Where's it from? It's from ______________ .

3 This flag is red, white and blue. Where's it from? It's from ______________ .

3 Now describe the flag of YOUR country.

____

____

____

4 Read and complete using the words from the box. Then listen and check.

9

think	Greece	know	where	color

Maria [1] ______________ are you from, Alisha?
Alisha I'm from [2] ______________ .
Maria What color is the Greek flag? I don't [3] ______________ .
Alisha It's white and blue. I [4] ______________ it's beautiful! Is the Peruvian flag white and blue too?
Maria No, it isn't.
Alisha What [5] ______________ is it?
Maria It's red and white.

GO GET IT

verb to be (int.) & short answers

5 Look at the Language Login. Complete and answer the questions.

1 ________ the German flag red and white?
No, ______________ .
2 ________ Charlotte Japanese?
No, ______________ . She's British.
3 ________ you from Portugal?
No, ______________ .
4 ________ the Brazilian flag green, yellow, blue and white?
Yes, ______________ .
5 ________ Juan from Puerto Rico?
Yes, ______________ .
6 ________ Giovanni Argentinian?
No, ______________ .

LANGUAGE LOGIN

Verb to be: Int. & short answers

Affirmative
You **are** from Greece.

Question	Short answers
Are you from Greece?	→ Yes, I **am**. / No, I'**m** not.
Is *the Greek flag* white and blue?	→ Yes, it **is**.
Is *the Japanese flag* white and blue?	→ No, it **isn't**.
Is *Madonna* American?	→ Yes, she **is**.
Is *Zac Efron* British?	→ No, he **isn't**.

PRACTICE

6 There's a mistake in each sentence. Find it and rewrite the sentences correctly. Follow the model.

1 You are from Mexico?
Are you from Mexico?
2 The Japanese flag red and white.
____
3 Where is you from?
____
4 I from Portugal.
____
5 Is Gisele Bündchen from Brazilian?
____

7 Look at the flags on page 9 and test your friend.

A Is the French flag red, white and blue?
B Yes, it is. / No, it isn't.

READING

1 **This is Mark's profile for his school site. Read and then listen to it.**

10

PROFILE · SCRAPS · PHOTOS · FANS · VIDEOS

Mark

My name's Mark. I'm 12 years old and my birthday is in May. I'm from Texas. My favorite color is black. My e-mail address is mjk@lol.com and my phone number is 356-7711.

I study at Green Valley School in class 4B. My favorite sport is soccer.

Lesson 4

COMPREHENSION

2 **Mark's talking to a new friend at school. Match the question to his answers.**

1 When is your birthday? [ ] It's mjk@lol.com

2 How old are you? [ ] It's 356-7711.

3 What's your e-mail address? [ ] It's in May.

4 What's your phone number? [ ] I'm twelve.

> **Tip**
> Saying your e-mail:
> athena@adelphe.net
> @ → at
> . → dot

VOCABULARY WORK

months of the year

3 **Write the months in the correct order. Then listen and repeat.**

11

April • May • November • December • September • February • August • March • January • October • July • June

GO GET IT

in + month

4 **Look at the Language Login. Circle the correct words to complete the sentences.**

1 My birthday is **in / from** December.
2 My e-mail address is **∅ / in** crpc@lupm.net.
3 In Brazil, classes start **in / ∅** February.
4 My friend's birthday is **∅ / in** July.

LANGUAGE LOGIN

Question words & preposition *in* + month

What's your e-mail address? ➜ It's darien@adelphe.net
What's your phone number? ➜ It's 6666-5555.
When is your birthday? ➜ My birthday is *in* March.
How do you spell your name? ➜ Z – A – C.

PRACTICE

5 **Unscramble the questions.**

is **birthday** **your** **When** **?**
1 ______________________________
My birthday is in ______________________________

is **What** **phone number** **your** **?**
2 ______________________________
It's ______________________________

is **e-mail address** **What** **your** **?**
3 ______________________________
It's ______________________________

are **you** **How old** **?**
4 ______________________________
I'm ______________________________

6 **Go back to #5. Answer the questions about YOU.**

LOG IN

7 **Writing.**
Write YOUR profile. Use #1 as a model. Share with your classmates.

Want more?
Go to Grammar Log - G1 (p. 89)

1 **Have a spelling contest. Ask about:**

nationalities	countries	months	your friend's name	colors

A How do you spell FRANCE?
B F – R – A – C – E.
A No, sorry. Try again.
B F – R – A – N – C – E.
A That's right!

2 **Answer the questions following the model.**

1 

Where's Paulo from?

He's from Chile.

2 

Is Grace Brazilian?

3 

When is Tanaka's birthday?

4 

How old is Giulia?

3 **Answer the questions below as fast as you can.**

1 Is the Canadian flag red and blue? ____________________
2 Is Shrek an ogre? ____________________
3 Is the Olympic flag yellow, red, black, green, blue and white? ____________________
4 Is Jack Sparrow a basketball player? ____________________
5 Is David Beckham German? ____________________
6 Is Avril Lavigne Canadian? ____________________

4 **Complete the text from the website virtual life.**

My name is Akemi. I'm an avatar. My [1] ______ is Ansha. I'm 16 [2] ______ old.

I'm [3] ______ China. My [4] ______ color is blue. My birthday is [5] ______ August. My e-mail [6] ______ is akemi@virtuallife.net.

5 **Interview Akemi. Write the questions to her answers.**

You ________________
Akemi Akemi Ansha.
You ________________
Akemi A – N – S – H – A.
You ________________
Akemi I'm 16.
You ________________
Akemi I'm from China.
You ________________
Akemi It's blue. I love blue.
You ________________
Akemi In August.
You ________________
Akemi It's akemi@virtuallife.net.
You Thank you.

Want more?
Go to Word Log - Unit 1 (p. 97)

6 **Rewrite the sentences using *he, she* or *it*.**

1 The French flag is red, white and blue.

____

2 Lucy's 14 years old.

____

3 Francesco is Italian.

____

Unit 2

Talking about myself and others

Lesson 1

VOCABULARY WORK

parts of the body

1 **Look at the picture. Write the correct number next to the parts of the body.**

- nose
- hand
- arm
- leg
- mouth
- foot
- ear
- hair
- eye

READING & COMPREHENSION

2 **Bob and Delia are e-pals. Delia is reading Bob's e-mail about his best friend Juan. Complete the table.**

12

Folders
Inbox
Friends
Spam
Trash
Sent Mail

To: deliaV778@dial.com
From: bob435@dial.com
Subject: Hi

Dear Delia,

Hi! How are you? My name is Robert Gibbons but call me Bob. I'm from Sydney, Australia. I'm 11 years old. How old are you?
I'm not tall. My hair is blond and my eyes are brown. I'm intelligent (I think!).
My best friend is Juan. He isn't Australian. He's from Puerto Rico. He's 12 years old. He's very tall and strong. His hair is brown. His eyes aren't brown. They're green. And he's very funny! We are very good friends.
Who's your best friend?
I love anime. I think it's very interesting. What about you?

Write soon! Bye!

Your e-pal,
Bob

name	e-mail	age	nationality	interests
Bob	______	______	______	______
Juan	juan_pr@virt.com	______	Puerto Rican	computer games

LANGUAGE LOGIN

Verb to be: neg.

I'm short.	→	I **am not** tall.	=	I'**m not** tall.
You're...	→	You **are not**	=	You **aren't**
He's...	→	He **is not**	=	He **isn't**
She's...	→	She **is not**	=	She **isn't**
We're...	→	We **are not**	=	We **aren't**
They're...	→	They **are not**	=	They **aren't**

GO GET IT

verb to be (neg.)

5 **Read the text in # 2 again. Complete the paragraph about Bob. Use the Language Login as reference.**

Bob's last name [1] __isn't__ Simpsom. It's Gibbons. Bob [2] ________ Greek. He's Australian. He [3] ________ 14. He [4] ________ tall. His hair [5] ________ blond. His eyes [6] ________ blue. They're brown. Bob and Delia are e-pals.

VOCABULARY WORK

adjectives

3 **Look at the highlighted adjectives in #2. Complete the chart about Bob and Juan.**

Name	Physical characteristics	Personality
Bob	not ________ ________ hair ________ eyes	________
Juan	tall and strong ________ hair ________ eyes	________
You	________ ________ hair ________ eyes	________

4 **Now go back to #3 and complete the chart about YOU.**

PRACTICE

6 **Complete the sentences using *we* or *they*.**

1 Superman and Spiderman are superheroes. ________ are very strong.

2 Mary and I are in class 5C. ________ are friends.

3 You and I are champions. ________ are very strong.

4 Harry Potter and Ron Weasley aren't real people. ________ are characters from J. K. Rowling stories.

VOCABULARY WORK

sports

1 Find TEN sports and write the words in the correct places.

SUETCYCLINGGOSHJDSOCCERMKHANGGLIDINGSOD

HJSKATEBOARDINGKDSIPDNVOLLEYBALLJSIPDMMCHDSURFING

MDKSBASKETBALLSKDNSWIMMINGHSJSJDYFBTENNISHSUTEFJUDO

PRACTICE

2 Answer the questions about YOU.

1 What's your favorite sport? My favorite sport is ________________________ .

2 Who's your favorite athlete? My favorite athlete is ________________________ .

Lesson 2

LANGUAGE LOGIN

Verb to be

Affirmative	Negative	Interrogative	Short answers	
I'**m**...	I'**m not**	**Am** I...?	Yes, you **are**.	No, you **aren't**.
You'**re**...	You **aren't**	**Are** you...?	Yes, I **am**.	No, I'**m not**.
He'**s**...	He **isn't**	**Is** he...?	Yes, he **is**.	No, he **isn't**.
She'**s**...	She **isn't**	**Is** she...?	Yes, she **is**.	No, she **isn't**.
We'**re**...	We **aren't**	**Are** we...?	Yes, we **are**.	No, we **aren't**.
They'**re**...	They **aren't**	**Are** they...?	Yes, they **are**.	No, they **aren't**.

GO GET IT

verb to be

3 **Two friends are talking about people they like. Look at the Language Login and complete the dialogue. Then listen and check.**

13

Tina Wow! Look at this picture! It's Orlando Bloom in his new movie.

Chris Cool! [1] __Is__ he American?

Tina No, he [2] ______. He's from England.

Chris [3] ______ he your favorite movie star?

Tina No, he isn't. My favorite movie star [4] ______ Daniel Radcliffe. I think he's great!

Chris And who's your favorite athlete?

Tina I'm not sure. I love Cristiano Ronaldo, Roger Federer and Bob Burnquist.

Chris [5] ______ they all American?

Tina Gee, Chris. Get real! Cristiano Ronaldo [6] ______ a Portuguese soccer player, Roger Federer [7] ______ a fantastic Swiss tennis player and Bob Burnquist [8] ______ a great Brazilian skateboarder! Come here. Let me show you some of their pictures.

Chris Great idea.

READING & COMPREHENSION

4 **Read the dialogue again. Who would say these sentences? Write T for *Tina* and C for *Chris*.**

1 [ ] Who is Cristiano Ronaldo?
2 [ ] I think Daniel is fantastic!
3 [ ] Look. This is Cristiano Ronaldo and this is Roger Federer.
4 [ ] I'm not really interested in sports.

PRACTICE

5 **Sports Quiz. Complete the questions and answers.**

1 ______ Thiago Pereira a swimmer?
Yes, ______.
2 ______ Robinho and Luis Figo soccer players?
Yes, ______.
3 ______ Pete Sampras a basketball player?
______. He's a tennis player.
4 ______ Kelly Slater and Dru Adler skateboarders?
No, ______. ______ surfers.
5 ______ Diego Hipólito a cyclist?
______. ______ a gymnast.

Want more?
Go to Grammar Log - G2 (pp. 89 & 90)

LOG IN

6 **Practice with a classmate.**
Create YOUR own sports quiz. On a piece of paper make up FIVE questions about your favorite athletes. Give them to three classmates to answer.

READING

1 **These are *X-Men* characters. Do you know who they are?**

Who is saying these lines? Read and learn their names.

[   ] He's Cyclops. He isn't short. He's tall and slim. His eyes are powerful.
[1] I'm Wolverine. He's Professor Charles Xavier. He's very intelligent. I'm his friend.
[   ] She's Phoenix. Her face is really beautiful!
[   ] She's Storm. Her hair is white and she's very strong.

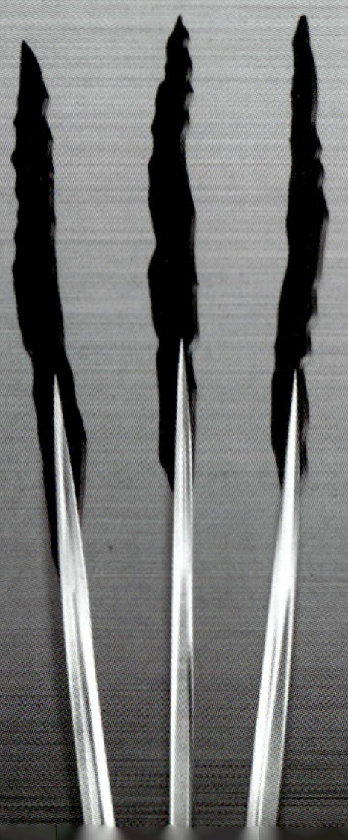

GO GET IT

his & her

2 **Look at the Language Login. Write about these *X-Men* characters. Use *he*, *she*, *his* or *her*.**

[1] Her name's Mystique. [2] ______'s blue. [3] ______ hair is short and red. [4] ______ eyes are green. [5] ______'s bad! [6] His name's Magneto. [7] ______ hair is gray and [8] ______ eyes are blue. [9] ______'s bad, too.

Mystique

PRACTICE

3 Complete the sentences using *I*, *he*, *she*, *my*, *his* or *her*. Then listen and check. 14

LANGUAGE LOGIN

Possessive adjectives

I'm a singer. **My** eyes are brown.
He's my friend. **His** eyes are green.
She's beautiful. **Her** hair is long.

4 Read the description of the picture above. Copy the sentences in the correct place.

Her eyes are brown. | His favorite *X-Men* character is Wolverine. | his hair is dark brown. | She's my best friend.

Those are my friends Gus and Yoko. Yoko's Japanese. [1] ___She's my best friend___ . She's tall and slim. [2] ________________ . Gus is a good friend too. His eyes are brown and [3] ________________ . He's an *X-Men* fan. [4] ________________ .

LOG IN

5 **Writing.**
Describe **YOUR** favorite adventure movie character. Follow the models in #3.

VOCABULARY WORK

adjectives

1 Learn the opinion adjectives below with the help of your teacher or a dictionary. Classify them. Then listen and repeat.

15

~~awesome~~	great
~~beautiful~~	intelligent
~~boring~~	interesting
cute	nice
fantastic	~~OK~~
friendly	rude
funny	weird
gorgeous	ugly

+		−
awesome	OK	boring
beautiful		

PRACTICE

2 Look at the pictures. Choose TWO adjectives from #1 to describe these people.

Nelson Mandela
Civil rights leader

______
______

JIM CARREY
Actor

______
______

ISABEL ALLENDE
Writer

great
intelligent

Lars Grael
Athlete

______
______

3 Now **YOU** write sentences using elements from #1 and #2.

Example: I think Isabel Allende is a great Chilean writer. She's intelligent.

1 ______

2 ______

Vocabulary Box

A I think Isabel Allende's great!
B I agree.
I don't agree.

Lesson 4

GO GET IT

our & their

4 Look at the Language Login box and complete with *our* or *their*.

Tip

In English we call our teachers by their last names: Mr. / Mrs. / Ms. / Miss + LAST NAME.

Example: Mr. Cruise, Miss Lopez, Mrs. Castro and Ms. Castello.

LANGUAGE LOGIN

Possessive adjectives

PRACTICE

5 Complete with *my*, *your*, *his*, *her*, *our* or *their*.

1 Mandela is awesome. _______ life is fantastic.

2 I think Mrs. Castro's great. She's _______ favorite teacher. She's beautiful: _______ hair is brown and _______ eyes are brown too.

3 George and David are best friends. _______ favorite sport is soccer.

4 Marcie and I are *X-Men* fans. _______ favorite character is Wolverine. We think he's awesome.

5 I know you! You're in class 3C and _______ name's Pablo, right?

Want more?
Go to Grammar Log - G3 (p. 90)

LOG IN

6 Writing.
Imagine you have a new teacher at school. Write an e-mail to a friend describing him / her. Use some of the adjectives from #1. Look at the e-mail on page 18 for reference.

e-mail

To:

From:

Subject: New teacher

____
(say hello / hi)

I have a new teacher at school. Her / His name's _______________________ .

He's / She's _______________________________________ .
(physical description)

I think _______________________________________ .
(your opinion)

See you!

____
(write your name)

Review

1 **Correct the sentences. Follow the model.**

1 Mike's hair is brown. (blond)
No, it isn't brown. It's blond.

2 Orlando Bloom is American. (British)

3 His best friend, Julia, is Canadian. (Italian)

4 Tina and Jessica are in class 3B. (2B)

5 You're a teacher. (student)

2 **Give true short answers about YOU.**

1 Are you from Canada? ______
2 Is your English teacher American? ______
3 Is your best friend 14 years old? ______
4 Are your classmates nice? ______
5 Is soccer your favorite sport? ______

3 **Fill in the blanks with *my*, *his*, *her*, *our* or *their*. Find Joanna, Sheila and Mike in the picture. Write their names.**

__My__ name's Joanna. [1] ______ hair is blond. [2] ______ eyes are blue. Sheila and Mike are my friends. [3] ______ favorite band is Evanescence. Sheila is tall and thin. [4] ______ hair is short. Mike is tall too. [5] ______ hair is long and red. We are classmates. [6] ______ school is in San Diego.

4 **Add as many words as you can to each category. You have three minutes.**

Sports	
Parts of the body	
Colors	
Countries	
Adjectives of opinion	

5 **Make FIVE sentences using some of the words from #4.**

1 ______________________________

2 ______________________________

3 ______________________________

4 ______________________________

5 ______________________________

6 **Read Rachel's school project on her favorite band and singer. Choose the correct options to complete her text.**

McFLY

by Rachel Anderson

My favorite band is McFly. They're from [1] ________ . Danny Jones [2] ________ my favorite McFly member. [3] ________ is a great singer. [4] ________ favorite sport is soccer, and his favorite female singers [5] ________ Eva Cassidy and Alanis Morissette. I think McFly is [6] ________ .

	a	b	c
1	British	Britain	british
2	aren't	are	is
3	He	She	It
4	Our	His	Her
5	am	is	are
6	boring	horrible	awesome

Want more?
Go to Word Log - Unit 2 (p. 98)

Unit 3

My things

Lesson 1

READING

1 Look at the picture and read the description of these two friends. Who is Julia and who is Rachel?

16

Julia and Rachel are friends. Julia's Brazilian. She's short and her hair is dark brown. She's an exchange student at the International School in Atlanta. Atlanta is the capital city of the state of Georgia in the USA. Rachel's African-American. She's tall and her hair is black. She's very intelligent. She helps Julia with her English.

GO GET IT

demonstrative pron. & ind. articles

2 **Rachel is helping Julia learn new words. Look at the Language Login and complete the dialogue. Use *this*, *that*, *a* or *an*.**

LANGUAGE LOGIN

Demonstrative pronouns: this / that & Indefinite articles: a / an

What's **this**?

It's **a** calculator.

It's **an** eraser.

What's **that**?

It's **a** desk.

It's **an** electronic organizer.

Attention! Use **an** before a vowel sound. Use **a** before a consonant sound. Use **this** to show an object / person near you. Use **that** to show an object / person that isn't near you.

VOCABULARY WORK

school objects

3 **Number the objects in the classroom.**

1 a desk
2 a whiteboard
3 a calculator
4 a computer
5 a pencil case
6 a mechanical pencil
7 a pen
8 an eraser
9 an electronic organizer
10 a book
11 a notebook

PRACTICE

4 **Listen, point to the objects in #3 and repeat.**

17

5 **What school objects do you have with YOU today?**

____

____

____

____

6 **Test your classmate. Follow the model.**

A What's this?
B It's an eraser.
A That's right.
B What's that?
A It's a pen.
B No, sorry. Try again.

Lesson 2

VOCABULARY WORK

personal objects

1 **Match the words to the pictures.**

[ ] a lipstick
[ ] a wallet
[ ] MP3 players
[ ] backpacks
[ ] cell phones
[ ] key rings
[ ] glasses

READING & COMPREHENSION

2 **Tom and Evelyn are talking about Lydia's objects. Read the cartoon strip and do the exercise.**

18

Write T for *true*, F for *false* or ? for *I don't know*.

[ ] Lydia's cell phone is pink.
[ ] Tom's glasses are pink.
[ ] Evelyn and Tom are friends.
[ ] These kids are at school.

LANGUAGE LOGIN

Demonstrative pronouns: these / those

What are **these**?
They're Lydia's key rings.

What are **those**?
They're Lydia's glasses.

Possessive 's

Put **'s** after singular nouns and people's names.

This is Clara.
It's **her** cell phone. → It's Clara**'s** cell phone.

This is Lucas.
It's **his** cell phone. → It's Lucas**'s** cell phone.

Attention! Use **these** to show objects / people near you.
Use **those** to show objects / people that aren't near you.

GO GET IT

these & those

3 Look at the Language Login. Complete the dialogues with the words in the box.

they (2x)	're	these (2x)	those

1 What are ____________ ?
____________'re erasers.

2 What are ____________ ?
They' ____________ MP3 players.

3 What are ____________ ?
____________'re wallets.

PRACTICE

4 Point at the objects in #3 and ask.

A What are these?
B They're key rings. What's this?
A It's a wallet.

5 Look at the objects in #1. Are they Tom's or Lydia's? What do YOU think?

6 Make a list of the personal objects YOU have in your backpack. Which one is your favorite?

____

____

____

Want more?
Go to Grammar Log - G4 (p. 91)

Lesson 3

READING

1 **Read and complete the dialogue with the words from the box. Then listen and check.**

19

these (2x)	that	those (2x)

Tim	Let's have a garage sale, Sam.
Sam	Great idea. [1] These are my posters.
Tim	Cool. What are [2] ________ ?
Sam	They're my old Matchbox cars.
	What are [3] ________ ?
Tim	They're my sister's stuffed animals.
Sam	And what's [4] ________ ?
Tim	It's an umbrella, my mom's umbrella.
Sam	Hey, [5] ________ are great roller skates.
Tim	Yes, they are fantastic!
Sam	Can I borrow your roller skates?
Tim	No way! It's a garage sale, Sam. Money, please!

VOCABULARY WORK

objects

2 **Look at the picture in #1. Number the words.**

[ ] an umbrella
[ ] Matchbox cars
[ ] posters
[ ] stuffed animals
[ ] roller skates

COMPREHENSION

3 **Read the dialogue again. Answer the questions. Follow the model.**

1 Are the posters Tim's? No, they aren't. They're Sam's.
2 Is the umbrella Sam's? No, it isn't.
3 Are the Matchbox cars Tim's? ________
4 Are the roller skates Sam's? ________

GO GET IT

let's

4 **Look at the Language Login. Find a suggestion in the dialogue in #1. Circle it.**

LANGUAGE LOGIN

Making suggestions: Let's

PRACTICE

5 **Put the words in order to make a dialogue.**

Sam	these / are / what / ?	What are these?
Tim	my / they / are / games / video / .	
Sam	cool / they / think / are / I / .	
Tim	play / let's / a / game / !	
Sam	idea / great / !	

LOG IN

6 **Practice with a classmate.**
Now YOU make suggestions. Use the prompts given.

Let's
- have a garage sale.
- play soccer.
- listen to a CD.
- play a computer game.
- watch TV.
- go skateboarding.

- ✓ Good idea!
- ✓ Great idea!
- ✗ No, sorry!
- ✗ Oh, no. Let's do something else!

READING

1 Read the paragraphs and match them to the pictures.

20

1

Hi. I'm Ginny. I'm from Indianapolis, Indiana, in the USA. I'm tall and slim. My hair's brown and my eyes are brown too. My school is called Green Hill and my classmates are great, especially the girls. Some boys at school are horrible. They're rude. They think they're funny, but they aren't.

2

Hello. My name's Edward but my friends call me Eddie. I'm 12 and I'm from Denver, in the state of Colorado in the USA. I'm not very tall but I'm strong. My hair is brown and my eyes are brown too. My friends from school are awesome. We play computer games and go skateboarding together. The girls are beautiful but they're boring. And they aren't soccer fans! I'm a big fan.

3

Hey, I'm David. I'm not American. I'm from Canada but my home is in Seattle, Washington, in the USA. I'm 13 and I'm very tall. My eyes are blue. I play basketball on the school team. I play the guitar, too. My classmates are fantastic. The boys are funny and we play ball games together. The girls are cute and intelligent. We listen to music and play computer games together.

COMPREHENSION

2 **Read the profiles again. Complete the sentences using the verb *to be* in the affirmative or negative form.**

1 Ginny __________ short.
2 In Ginny's opinion, boys __________ funny.
3 Eddie __________ 12 and he's American.

LANGUAGE LOGIN

Conjunctions: and & but

The girls are cute **and** intelligent.
They think they're funny, **but** they aren't.

Attention! Use **and** to link similar ideas.
Use **but** to link contrasting ideas.

3 **Read the sentences below. Which text could they belong to? Check (✓) the text number.**

		text 1	text 2	text 3
1	They're OK. Our team is called "The East Warriors".	○	○	○
2	Some boys are interesting.	○	○	○
3	I love soccer. It's my favorite sport.	○	○	○
4	I play sports, but I love music. I play a musical instrument, too.	○	○	○

GO GET IT

and & but

4 **Look at the Language Login. Match the sentences.**

1 Eddie's from Denver and — [ ] his mom isn't. She's from France.
2 Ginny's hair is brown and — [ ] his best friend is from Denver too.
3 David's Canadian but — [ ] the girls at his school aren't.
4 Eddie's a soccer fan but — [ ] her eyes are brown.

PRACTICE

5 **Make THREE sentences. Follow the model.**

Ginny is tall
She thinks boys are rude
Eddie isn't tall
Eddie thinks girls are boring
David is from Canada

and
but

slim.
he's strong.
beautiful.
his home is in Seattle.
boring.

Examples: Ginny is tall and slim. Eddie isn't tall but he's strong.

1 ______________________________
____
2 ______________________________
____
3 ______________________________
____

LOG IN

6 **Writing.**
In your notebook write YOUR profile for your blog. Use the paragraphs in #1 as models.

- Say who you are (name, age, nationality).
- Describe yourself.
- Talk about your school and school friends.

1 **Unscramble the letters. Write the words and the correct articles.**

1. D R A O B I T W H E — a whiteboard
2. L A B M R U L E — ______ ______
3. B K A A P C C K — ______ ______
4. R G I A N O E Z O E R R L I C N T E C — ______ ______
5. R A E S R E — ______ ______
6. A L S T C A U O L C — ______ ______

2 **In your notebook, write TWO sentences using words from #1.**

3 **Look at the pictures and complete the dialogues.**

4 **Unscramble the words.**

1 those / Alice's / are / glasses / ? ______

2 Matt's / cell phone / that's / . ______

3 movies / the / let's / to / go / . ______

4 this / Clark's / is / mechanical pencil / ? ______

5 are / these / key rings / Antony's / . ______

6 is / what / that / ? ______

5 **Complete the sentences. Use the words below.**

funny	charming	handsome	intelligent	strong
ugly	weird	friendly	beautiful	boring

1 Gisele Bündchen's ______ and ______.

2 Avril Lavigne's ______, but ______.

3 Ronaldinho Gaúcho's ______, but ______.

4 Johnny Depp's ______ and ______.

5 Ben Stiller's ______ and ______.

6 **Complete the questions. Use: *what*, *where* and *how old*.**

1 ______'s your full name?

2 ______ are you?

3 ______'s your e-mail address?

4 ______ are you from?

5 ______'s your favorite color?

6 ______ is your friend?

Want more?
Go to Word Log - Unit 3 (p. 98)

LOG IN

7 **Practice with a classmate.**
Ask and answer questions. Fill in the card.

Full name	______
Age	______
E-mail address	______
Country	______
Favorite color	______

Unit 4

My school & neighborhood

Lesson 1

READING & COMPREHENSION

1 Read the Town Hill School site and check the corresponding floor plan.

21

Town Hill School

TOWN HILL SCHOOL

ABOUT THS   BOARD OF EDUCATION   PARENTS & STUDENTS   TEACHERS & STAFF   COMMUNITY & GOVERNMENT

THS RESOURCES
- news & events
- calendars
- newsletter
- public notices

- departments
- forms
- initiatives/programs

- school description
- school enrollment
- athletics
- interactive map
- lesson plans & students work

- site map

SCHOOL DESCRIPTION

Town Hill is located in Philadelphia, Pennsylvania. The school is 60 years old. On the first floor there is a library, an auditorium, a cafeteria, a science lab and a computer lab, a gym, a health office and administrative offices. Outside there is a playing field. On the second floor, there are 10 classrooms and many bathrooms. There are approximately 150 students at Town Hill and 20 teachers.

Most students are involved in extracurricular activities, including foreign language classes (Spanish and French), sports activities (football, soccer, basketball, ice skating and hockey), drama and music classes. There is a group of six support teachers to help students and the principal's office is open to students at all times.

There is a subway station near the school and other facilities such as a mall and a supermarket.

LINKS

ADMINISTRATIVE
Ms. Sherry Hunter, Principal

SARC
School Profile
Academic Plan
ADA Access Guide
Website

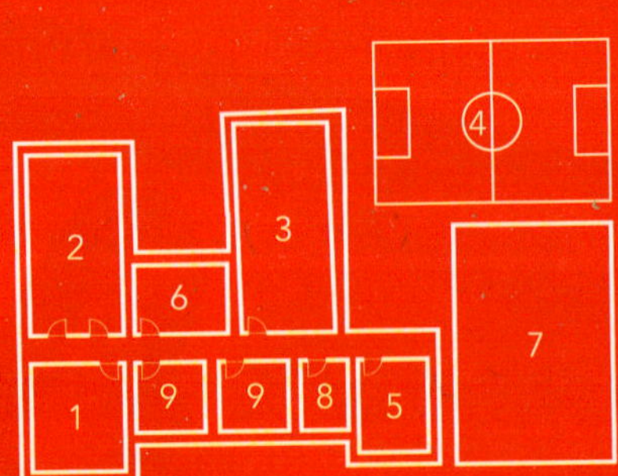

1st floor

1 library
2 auditorium
3 cafeteria
4 playing field
5 science lab
6 computer lab
7 gym
8 health office
9 administrative offices

Floor plan 1

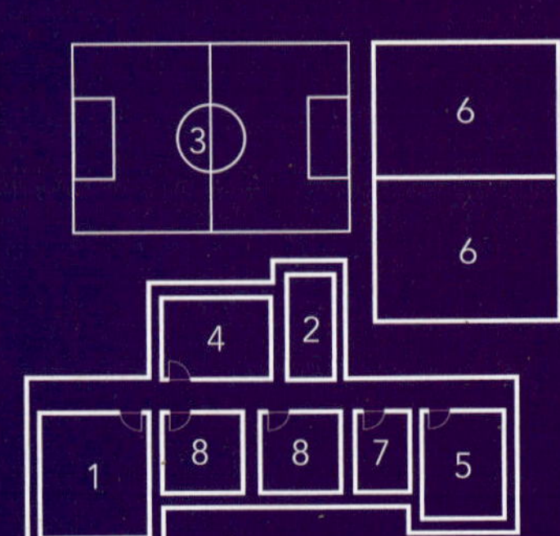

1st floor

1 library
2 cafeteria
3 playing field
4 science lab
5 computer lab
6 gym
7 health office
8 administrative offices

Floor plan 2

LANGUAGE LOGIN

There is & There are

Singular → **There is** = **There's** an auditorium.

Plural → **There are** ten classrooms on the second floor.

VOCABULARY WORK

at school

2 **Look at the highlighted words in #1. With the help of your teacher or a dictionary, group the words according to the categories below.**

People	students,
School facilities	a library,
Sports	football,
Extracurricular activities	foreign languages,
Neighborhood facilities	a subway station,

GO GET IT

there is & there are

3 **Look at the Language Login. Complete the sentences about Town Hill School with *there is* or *there are.***

At Town Hill School...

1 There is a gym next to the science lab.
2 ______ six support teachers.
3 ______ a computer lab with 20 new computers.
4 ______ an auditorium for 100 people.
5 ______ a library on the first floor.

PRACTICE

4 **Look at the floor plan 2 in #1. Make sentences. Follow the model.**

1 (cafeteria) There's a cafeteria.
2 (gym) ______
3 (library) ______
4 (offices) ______

5 **Write about YOUR school.**

school name ______

In my school there are ______ classrooms.

There's ______ and ______.

Near my school there's a library, auditorium, bookstore, reception.

and there are playgrounds, classrooms, computer lab, ______.

VOCABULARY WORK

objects

1 **Bob's a Town Hill School student. He's very disorganized. Look at his bedroom. How many objects can you name? Number them.**

1 a cell phone
2 an MP3 player
3 CDs
4 a mechanical pencil
5 a diary
6 glasses
7 a backpack
8 a desk
9 sneakers
10 a chair
11 a window
12 a bed

READING & LISTENING

2 **Bob is in his bedroom talking to his friend Linda. Read and listen to their dialogue. Circle the words you hear.**

22

Linda	We're late, Bob. Let's go!
Bob	OK. Let me just get my stuff from my bedroom. This is my room, Linda. Come in.
Linda	What a mess!
Bob	Yeah, sorry! Let me get my cell phone. It's... Where's my cell phone?
Linda	It's [1] **on / behind** the laptop. And your diary is [2] **behind / next to** it.
Bob	My backpack, where is it? Ah, it's there [3] **between / in** the desk and the chair.
Linda	What's that [4] **next to / under** the window?
Bob	It's my MP3 player. Oh, there. My glasses are [5] **next to / behind** the laptop.
Linda	I don't believe it, Bob! Your CDs are [6] **between / in** your sneaker! That's disgusting!
Bob	I don't mind. Let's find my mechanical pencil and go to school. It's right here, [7] **under / next to** these books. Let's go.

COMPREHENSION

3 **Check (✓) the right answer.**

1 What's Linda's opinion of Bob's bedroom?
- ◯ It's beautiful!
- ◯ It's OK.
- ◯ It's horrible.

2 Where are they going?
- ◯ To Bob's bedroom.
- ◯ To school.
- ◯ To the mall.

LANGUAGE LOGIN

Where & Prepositions of place

Where's my cell phone?

It's **on** the box.

It's **in** the box.

It's **under** the box.

Where are the CDs?

They are **behind** the box.

They are **next to** the box.

They are **between** the boxes.

Where's Bob's scho

It's **near** his hous

VOCABULARY WORK

expressions

4 **Find the expressions in the dialogue. What do they mean? Match them to their meaning below.**

1 What a mess!
2 I don't mind.
3 That's disgusting!

[ ] It isn't important to me.
[ ] It's horrible! It's gross!
[ ] Your room isn't organized. It isn't tidy.

GO GET IT

where & prepositions of place

5 **Look at the Language Login. Complete the questions and answers about Bob's bedroom.**

1 ___Where's___ his MP3 player?
It's ___under___ the window.
2 ______ his glasses?
They're ______ the laptop.
3 ______ his backpack?
It's ______ the desk and the chair.
4 ______ his cell phone?
It's ______ the laptop.

PRACTICE

6 **Now Bob's room is clean! Where are these objects now?**

1 (his MP3 player)
It's on his bed.
2 (his glasses)
______
3 (his backpack)
______
4 (his CDs)
______

7 **What is YOUR classroom like? In your notebook, write a description for the school website.**

Example: There's a door between the whiteboard and the window.

Lesson 3

READING

1 **Jake and Susan are friends. They're talking about Susan's neighborhood. Complete their dialogue with *there is* or *there are*. Then listen and check.**

23

Jake	Susan, what do you think of your neighborhood?
Susan	Well, I think it's beautiful and calm. [1] There is a big park near my house.
Jake	Is there a mall?
Susan	No, there isn't. But [2] there are three stores next to the hospital.
Jake	Are there any movie theaters?
Susan	Yes, [3] there is one next to my school. But there aren't any restaurants.
Jake	Is there a cybercafé?
Susan	Oh, yes. That's my favorite place. And [4] there is a diner too.

COMPREHENSION

2 **Answer the questions.**

1 What's Susan's opinion about her neighborhood?
She thinks beautiful and calm

2 What's her favorite place?
her favorite place is Cybercaffé

3 Is there a green area near her house?
Yes There is

GO GET IT

there is / are & is there / are there...?

3 **Look at the Language Login. Complete the questions about Susan's neighborhood. Then answer them.**

1 Are there any libraries?
No, there aren't.

2 ______ a park?
______

3 ______ a hospital?
______

4 ______ any stores?
______

LANGUAGE LOGIN

There is / There are

Affirmative

Singular → **There's** a restaurant.

Plural → **There are** two stores.

Negative

There isn't a mall. = **There is no** mall.

There aren't any movie theaters. = **There are no** movie theaters.

Interrogative

Singular → **Is there** a mall?

Plural → **Are there** any stores?

Short answers

Yes, **there is**. No, **there isn't**.

Yes, **there are**. No, **there aren't**.

PRACTICE

4 Unscramble the sentences.

1 aren't / there / stores / any / .
There aren't any stores

2 there / a / is / diner / ?
Is there a diner?

3 any / schools / there / are / ?
Are there any schools?

4 two / malls / are / there / .
There are two malls.

5 What is there in YOUR neighborhood? Complete the THREE survey questions and answer them.

NEIGHBORHOOD SURVEY	Your neighborhood		Your classmate's neighborhood	
	Yes	No	Yes	No
1 ____________ a mall?				
2 ____________ any stores?				
3 ____________ a cybercafé?				
4 ____________				
5 ____________				
6 ____________				

LOG IN

6 Practice with a classmate.
Go back to #5 and complete the survey with THREE more questions. Interview a classmate.

Want more?
Go to Grammar Log - G5 & G6 (pp. 91 & 92)

READING & COMPREHENSION

1 **Sandy isn't a student at Town Hill School anymore. Read her e-mail to her old friend Kim. Then check (✓) the correct options.**

24

MY NEW SCHOOL

To: kimb435@dial.com
From: sanV778@dial.com
Subject: My new school

new e-mail | reply | forward

Dear Kim,

Hi! How are you?

I love my new school here in Windermere, Florida! It's called Greyson Middle School.

The school is near my house. It's awesome! There are 10 classrooms and 20 teachers. There's an auditorium, a computer lab, a health office and a cafeteria. There's a gym and a playing field. The principal's office is next to my classroom. (This is a problem!)

My classroom is on the second floor. There are 12 boys and 15 girls in my class. My favorite teacher is the drama teacher. His name is Mr. Howard. He's tall and fat. He's very funny and intelligent.

What about Town Hill School? Are there any new teachers?

I miss you all. Write soon. Bye.

Sandy

download

attached file (283 Kb)

1 ◯ Sandy thinks her new school is fantastic.
2 ◯ Sandy and Kim are classmates at Greyson Middle School.
3 ◯ Mr. Howard's a drama teacher.

2 **Complete the form about Sandy's new school.**

School: Greyson Middle School
Location: ______
Number of classrooms: ______
Other school facilities: an auditorium, ______
Number of students in her class: ______
Favorite teacher: ______

Vocabulary Box

20 twenty
21 twenty-one
22 twenty-two
23 twenty-three
24 twenty-four
25 twenty-five
26 twenty-six
27 twenty-seven
28 twenty-eight
29 twenty-nine
30 thirty
31 thirty-one
...
37 thirty-seven
...
40 forty
...
49 forty-nine
50 fifty

LANGUAGE LOGIN

How many...? & Pronoun: none

How many classrooms **are there?** → There are ten classrooms.
How many teachers **are there?** → There are twenty teachers.
How many computer labs **are there?** → There's one. / **None**.

GO GET IT

how many...?

3 **Look at the Language Login. Ask questions for these answers.**

1 ____________ boys are there in your classroom? There are twenty.
2 ____________ windows ____________ in your room? There's one.
3 ______________________________ ?
None. There are no pens in my backpack. There's only a book.

PRACTICE

4 **There's a mistake in each sentence. Find it and rewrite the sentences correctly.**

1 How many cafeterias is there?
____

2 How many floors there are in your school?
____

3 There isn't store near my school.
____

4 How many office are there?
____

Want more?
Go to Grammar Log - G7 (p. 92)

LOG IN

5 **Writing.**
Complete the table about YOUR school and in your notebook write an e-mail to an old friend. Look at the model in #1 for help.

School	
Location	
Number of classrooms	
Other school facilities	
Number of students in your class	
Favorite teacher	

Review

1 **Look at the picture. Correct the underlined parts of the sentences below.**

1 cybercafé
2 supermarket
3 movie theather
4 stores
5 school
6 mall
7 hospital
8 restaurants

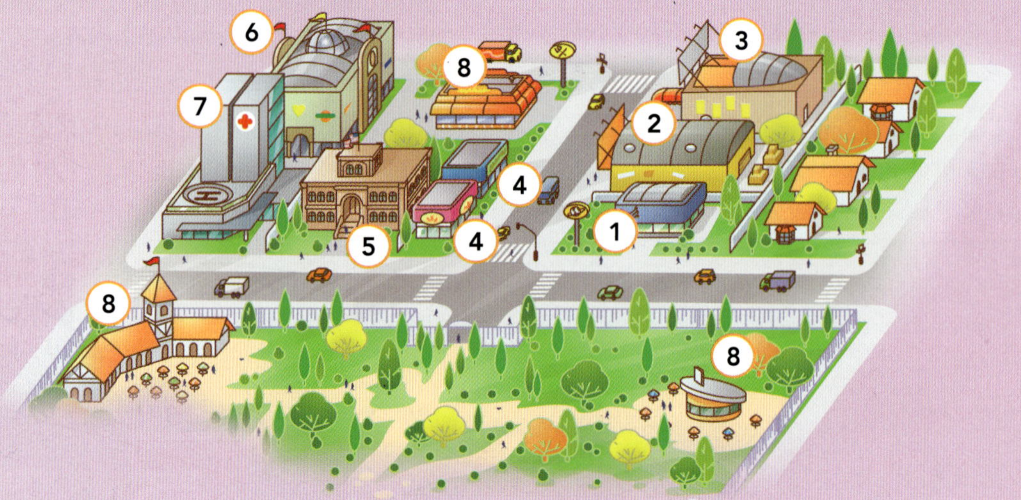

1 There's a school behind the hospital.
There's a school next to the hospital.

2 There are three restaurants in the park.
There's a restaurant in the park.

3 There's a subway station behind the hospital.
There's a mall behind the hospital

4 There's a supermarket between the park and the restaurant.
There's a supermarket between the movies theathers and cybercafé.

5 There aren't stores near the school.
There are stores near the school

2 **Sandra is describing her neighborhood. Read the paragraph and answer the questions.**

1 Is the park behind the school?
No, there isn't.

2 Where's the library?
The library.

3 How many stores are there?
There are two big stores.

4 Is there a cybercafé?
Yes, there is.

5 Where is it?
It's between the theather and park.

My neighborhood,
by Sandra Gann

I love my neighborhood. My school is next to the park. The subway station is behind my school. There's a cybercafé in the park. There are two big stores between the library and the supermarket.

3 **Listen and circle the numbers you hear.**

25

1 In Jessica's school there are **27 / 37** classrooms.
2 In Marco's school there are **35 / 55** students.
3 In Julian's class there are **20 / 30** boys.
4 In Fiona's neighborhood there are **32 / 33** stores.

4 **Write the words.**

1
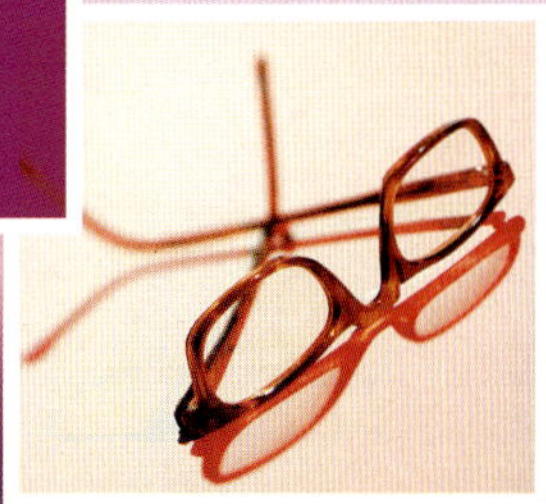

2

3

4

5

6

7

8

5 **Choose SIX words from #4 and write them in the squares. Play Battleship.**

A A3
B Glasses. Your point. C1.
C Water! My point!

Want more?
Go to Word Log - Unit 4 (p. 99)

	1	2	3
A			glasses
B			
C			
D			
E			

Unit 5

Families around the world

Lesson 1

READING & COMPREHENSION

1 26 **Read the article about Angelina Jolie's family and check (✓) the correct answers.**

CINEMA

Angelina Jolie is a gorgeous movie star, an international diplomat and an Oscar winner.

She has blue eyes and dark brown hair. Her movies are a great success! But Angelina is also the mother of three adopted children: Maddox, a Cambodian boy, Pax Thien, a Vietnamese boy, and Zahara Marley, an Ethiopian girl. She also has three kids with her husband Brad Pitt: Shiloh Nouvel and the twins Knox Leon and Vivienne Marcheline. Angelina is so happy as a mom that the family may get even bigger in the future...

Teens Magazine, 2008

1 Angelina Jolie's ◯ **married to** ◯ **divorced from** Brad Pitt.
2 Shiloh Nouvel is Angelina and Brad's ◯ **friend** ◯ **daughter**.
3 Brad is Maddox's ◯ **real father** ◯ **stepfather**.
4 Angelina is Shiloh's ◯ **real mother** ◯ **stepmother**.
5 Angelina has many ◯ **sons** ◯ **children**.

GO GET IT

possessive 's

2 Look at the Language Login. Complete the sentences using *'s* or *'*.

1 Maddox is Pax Thien 's brother.
2 This is my parents __ car.
3 Angelina is Zahara __ mother.
4 The boys __ bedroom is big.
5 Their parents __ house is comfortable.

Vocabulary Box

parents = father and mother
mother = mom / mommy
father = dad / daddy

VOCABULARY WORK

members of the family

3 Now read about another family, Sandy's family. Read the description and write people's names.

This is my family. My mom's name is Helen. She is divorced from Roger and married to my dad Phillip. Isabel and Charles are my mother's parents, and Miguel and Elizabeth are my father's parents. My grandparents are great! Suzie's my half sister. She's my mom and Roger's daughter. Scott and Sophie are my father's brother and sister. My uncle Scott is very funny! My aunt Sophie has two children, Oscar and Jane. They're my cousins.

LANGUAGE LOGIN

Possessive 's & '

Put **'s** after singular nouns and people's names.
Helen is Andy**'s** mother.

Attention! We use **'s** and **'** to indicate possession.
Put **'** after plural nouns.
Sophie is my cousins**'** mother.

PRACTICE

4 **Look at #3 again. Sandy is talking about her family. Use the prompts to write sentences. Follow the model.**

1 Isabel → Helen
Isabel is Helen's mother.

2 Phillip → my grandparents
____

3 Scott → my dad
____

4 Sophie → my cousins
____

5 Roger → Suzie
____

5 **Verb *to be* or *possessive 's*? Rewrite the sentences using *is* where appropriate.**

1 My sister's name's Celia.
My sister's name is Celia.

2 That's my brother's son.
____

3 My uncle's name's Robert.
____

4 My sister's best friend's French.
____

Lesson 2

READING & COMPREHENSION

1 **Before you read the article in #2, look at the picture. What do you know about this person? Write T for *true* and F for *false*.**

1 [ ] Her last name is Ciccone.
2 [ ] Madonna's an actress and a singer.
3 [ ] She's British.
4 [ ] She has three children.
5 [ ] She's married to Sean Penn.

2 **Now read about Madonna and check your answers in #1.**

27

MADONNA

Madonna Louise Ciccone is from the USA. She's a famous singer and actress. She has a daughter and two sons. She was married to Guy Ritchie, a British director. Her daughter's name is Lourdes. Guy isn't Lourdes's real father. Rocco John is Madonna and Guy's son. Madonna and Guy adopted David Banda. He's from Malawi. Lourdes and Rocco have a brother now. It's a big family!

VOCABULARY WORK

parts of the body

3 **Match the parts of the body below with the numbers in Madonna's picture.**

[ ] leg
[ ] arm
[ ] head
[ ] knee
[ ] neck
[ ] shoulder

Vocabulary Box

Mouth → tooth / teeth / tongue

Hand → finger(s)

Foot / Feet → toe(s)

LANGUAGE LOGIN

Have & has / Word order: color + noun

Lourdes **has** little brothers.
Madonna **has** blue eyes.
David and Rocco **have** a nice sister.
Madonna and Guy **have** a big family.

Attention!

Say I / you / we / they + **have**.
Say he / she / it + **has**.

In English, the **adjective** comes **before** the **noun**.
red hair / long legs / green eyes / a big family

GO GET IT

have & has / word order

4 Look at the Language Login. Check (✓) the correct option.

1 Madonna ◯ have ◯ has long legs.

2 Rocco and David ◯ have ◯ has a big sister.

3 Madonna and Guy ◯ have ◯ has one adopted child.

4 Lourdes ◯ has ◯ have brown hair.

5 My sister ◯ have ◯ has big hands.

5 Unscramble the sentences.

1 cousin / feet / my / ugly / has / .

____

2 has / Karla's / a / father / neck / long / .

____

3 teeth / have / yellow / smokers / .

____

LOG IN

6 Practice with a classmate.
Choose THREE members of YOUR family and describe them.

Example: Uncle Edward → My uncle is tall and strong. He has black hair and brown eyes. He has a big nose.

Want more?

Go to Grammar Log - G8 (p. 93)

LISTENING & READING

1 **Ivan is at home with his family. Listen, read and complete their conversation.** 28

Martha	Let's go out and have a picnic, guys. It's a [1] ____________ afternoon!
Ivan	Great idea!
Lisa	No way, Mom! I think picnics are stupid!
Ivan	What about a [2] ____________ game? There's one on TV.
Lisa	Oh no, please! I hate football!
Ivan	What's your suggestion then?
Lisa	What about going to the movies?
Martha	There are no good [3] ____________ on right now.
Ivan	Well, what about getting a [4] ____________ and watching it at home?
Lisa	OK, Dad! Another boring afternoon!

COMPREHENSION

2 **Correct the information in the sentences according to #1.**

1 Martha is Lisa's big sister.

____

2 There are good movies on at the moment.

____

3 Lisa's happy about watching a DVD at home.

____

GO GET IT

making suggestions

3 **Look at the Language Login. Make possible combinations. Write 1 or 2 in the second column.**

1 What about	[1] a soccer game?
2 Let's	[ ] a party?
	[ ] have a picnic.
	[ ] watch a DVD.
	[ ] a picnic?
	[ ] playing soccer?

PRACTICE

4 **Complete using *Let's...* or *What about...*?**

1 ______________________ swimming?
2 ______________________ go cycling.
3 ______________________ playing tennis?
4 ______________________ surfing?
5 ______________________ watch a movie.

LANGUAGE LOGIN

Making suggestions & giving responses

Let's go out and have a picnic!
Let's go swimming!
Let's play tennis.

What about a football game?
What about cycling?
What about playing basketball?

} **Great! / Good idea!**
I don't know!
No way!

Attention! **Let's** + verb
What about + noun or verb + ing

5 **Choose TWO suggestions from #4. Write their numbers and respond to them. What would YOU say?**

____

____

VOCABULARY WORK

go & play

6 **Write the words and expressions you know in the correct column. With the help of your teacher or a dictionary, learn the ones you don't know.**

go	play

soccer
to the park
on a picnic
cycling
sports
video games
football
for a walk
bowling

LOG IN

7 **Practice with a classmate.**
It's a holiday and you're happy. Make suggestions.
Accept or refuse them.
Use the vocabulary from #6.

VOCABULARY WORK

occupations

1 **Learn these occupations with the help of your teacher or a dictionary. Match the words and pictures.**

sales clerk • police officer • tour guide • nurse • flight attendant • architect • manager • ~~web designer~~

1 web designer

2

3

4

5

6

7

8

READING

2 **These are teens from different parts of the world. Read their blogs. Complete the sentences using *is, are, have* or *has*. Then listen and check.**

29

My name's **Dina**. I'm Brazilian.

My family's really small: it's me and my mom. My mother's name [1] ____________ Angela. She's tall and slim. She [2] ____________ brown eyes and her hair [3] ____________ black. She's beautiful. We live in a small apartment in Rio de Janeiro. There's only one bedroom and one bathroom. My mom's a secretary. We watch DVDs and go swimming together. I love my mom.

posted by Dina at 6:43 p.m. 564 comments.

My name's **Helen**. I'm American.

Our house [4] ____________ in New Jersey. My family is very big. I [5] ____________ 14 brothers and sisters. There [6] ____________ four bedrooms in our house. I have a twin brother. His name is John. He has short brown hair. My mom and my dad are lawyers. We're a happy family.

posted by Helen at 12:25 p.m. 398 comments.

COMPREHENSION

3 **Complete the table below according to the blogs in #2.**

	Brothers and sisters	People in the house / apartment	Parents' occupation
Dina	0 = none	2	secretary
Helen			
Liu Youyao			

LANGUAGE LOGIN

there is / are vs. have / has

There's only one bedroom in Dina's house.
Dina's house **has** only one bedroom.

There are twins in Helen's family.
Helen's parents **have** twins.

Attention! There's a lot of work there.
~~NOT~~ Has a lot of work there.

4 **Who is it? Write the correct names.**

1 Her hair is black and her eyes are brown.
Angela, Dina's mother

2 He has two cousins.
____

3 There are many bedrooms in her house.
____

4 He's short and strong.
____

GO GET IT

there is / are vs. have / has

5 **Look at the Language Login. Complete the sentences with *there's*, *there are*, *have* or *has*.**

1 __________ many animals on Liu Youyao's father's farm.

2 They __________ a lot of work on the farm.

3 Helen's house __________ four bedrooms.

4 __________ a secretary in Dina's family.

My name's Liu Youyao.
I'm Chinese.

I'm from a small village in China. My family's big. I (7) ________ four brothers. My brother Luo (8) ________ short but he's very strong. He (9) ________ intelligent too! We live in a small house with my mother, my father, my grandmother, my aunt, and two cousins. My mom and dad (10) ________ farmers. There's a lot of work on the farm.

posted by Liu Youyao at 4:30 p.m. 300 comments.

LOG IN

6 **Writing.**
First complete the table about YOU and your family.

	Write your name here.
Brothers and sisters	
People in the house / apartment	
Parents' occupation	

Then, in your notebook write a paragraph about your family for a website. Look at the models in #2 for help.

Review

1 **Complete the crosswords with the correct family members' words.**

1 My uncle's son is my...
2 My mother's mother is my...
3 My mother's brother is my...
4 My mother's sister is my...
5 My father's father is my...
6 My mom and stepfather's daughter is my...

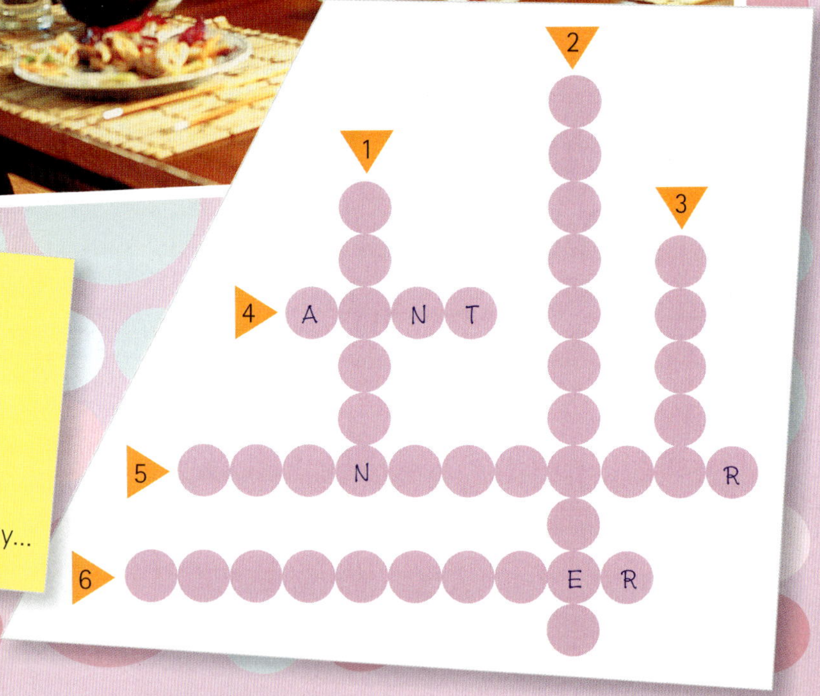

2 **Complete using 's or '.**

1 These are the girls___ backpacks.
2 That is Lucas___ MP4 player.
3 They are the boy___ grandparents.
4 They are the boys___ parents.
5 This is Suzie___ lipstick.

3 **Make suggestions.**

1 going / to the movies / ?

____

2 go / surfing / .

____

3 play / tennis / .

____

4 playing / volleyball / ?

____

4 **Unscramble the words. What are the occupations?**

1 ewb grdeinse ____________________

2 unsre ____________________

3 gaanmer ____________________

4 tcthcreia ____________________

5 rotu eugid ____________________

5 **Choose TWO words from #4. Write sentences using them.**

Example: My uncle is a manager.

1 ____

2 ____

6 **Complete this teen's blog using *have*, *has*, *there is* or *there are*.**

My name's Nicole. I [1] __________ a big family. [2] __________ seven people in my family: mom, dad, my grandma, two sisters, one little brother and I. My baby brother's cute, but he cries a lot. He [3] __________ brown eyes and blond hair. [4] __________ three bedrooms in our house and that's OK. The problem is that [5] __________ only one bathroom.

7 **Read the sentences. What are the missing words? Write them in the correct places.**

- We have many **?** in our mouth. _ _ _ _ H
- Spiders have eight **?** . L _ _ _
- We have one **?** in our mouth. _ O _ _ _ _
- Giraffes have long **?** . _ _ _ _ S
- We have toes on our **?** . _ E _ _
- We have a hand at the end of each **?** . _ R _

Want more?

Go to Word Log - Unit 5 (pp. 99 & 100)

Unit 6

Schools around the world

READING & COMPREHENSION

Lesson 1

1 Karen and Sally study at a school in the USA. They're talking about their new schedule. Read their dialogue and write T for *true* and F for *false*.

30

Sally	Karen, let's check our schedule for this year. Home economics with Mrs. Jones and Mathematics with Mr. Harris. Oh, I hate Math.
Karen	I like Math, but I don't like Mr. Harris. He's really boring.
Sally	Look, Geography with Mr. Richards, and History with Miss Samson. I love History and Miss Samson's just great!
Karen	Who's our Arts teacher?
Sally	Ms. Johnson. She's really nice. And we have Physical Education with Mr. Keyton. I love all sports. PE is my favorite subject.
Karen	It's my sister's favorite subject too but I hate it! Listen! Mr. Dunwell's our Science teacher! Awesome! That's my favorite subject!
Sally	And Mr. Dunwell is great!
Karen	I know!

Want more?
How do you spell *science*? Practice.

Vocabulary Box
Mathematics = Math
Physical Education = PE

1 [ ] Mr. Harris is the Math teacher.
2 [ ] Sally's favorite subject's Geography.
3 [ ] Karen likes Science.
4 [ ] The girls think Mr. Dunwell is boring.

VOCABULARY WORK

school subjects

2 Use the highlighted school subjects from #1 to complete the chart below.

Mrs. Seligson
English

Mr. Keyton
Physical Education ( )

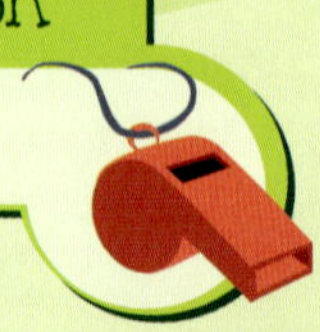

Mathematics ( )
Mr. Harris

LANGUAGE LOGIN

Likes & dislikes

I **love** Arts.

I **like** Math.

I **don't like** History.

I **hate** Science.

PRACTICE

4 **Complete with true information about YOU.**

A color you (love) : ______________________

A movie star you (like) : ______________________

A sport you (don't like) : ______________________

A singer you (hate) : ______________________

5 **In your notebook, write sentences using the information from #4.**

Example: I love blue.

Want more?
Go to Grammar Log - G9 (p. 93)

GO GET IT

verbs of likes & dislikes

3 **Look at Karen's notebook and at the Language Login. Then match her notes to the sentences.**

1 I love Science!
2 I like Math.
3 I don't like Mr. Harris.
4 I hate PE.

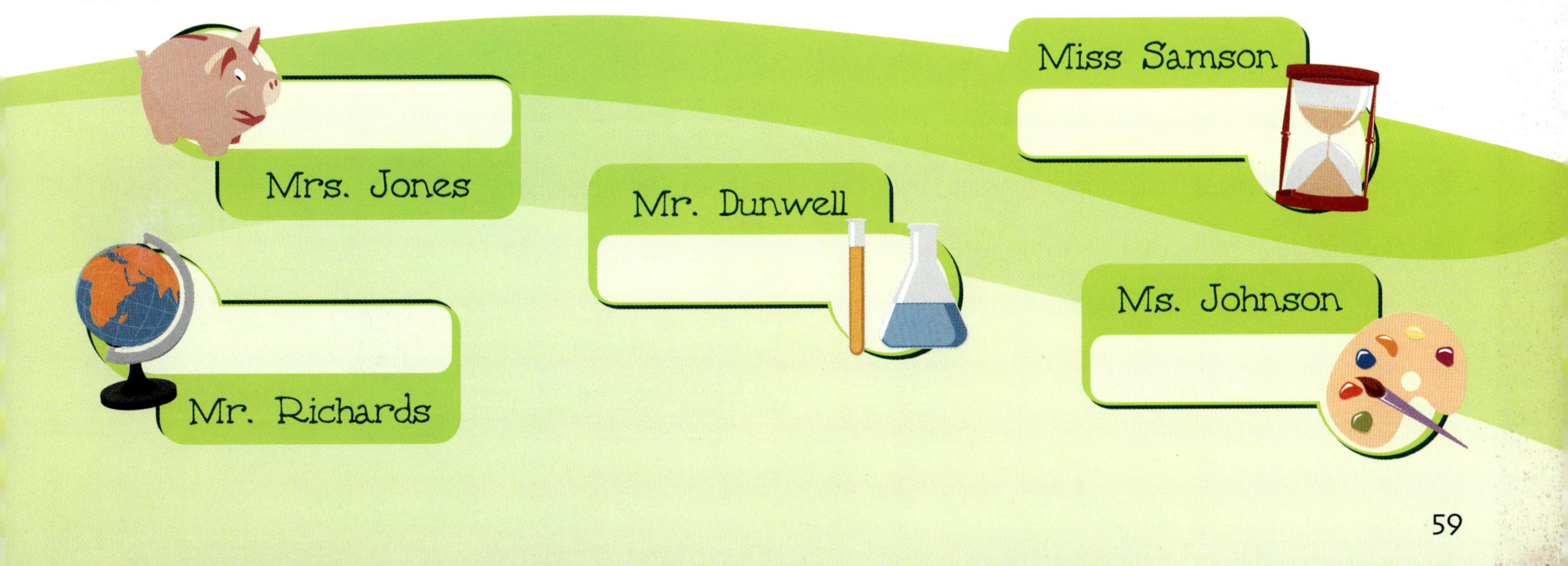

Lesson 2

READING & COMPREHENSION

1 31 **Read this descripton of Harry Potter's routine at Hogwarts School. Complete his schedule with the school subjects.**

Harry

This is Harry Potter. His best friends are Ron and Hermione. They study at Hogwarts School of Witchcraft and Wizardry. Hogwarts is a school of magic in the north of England. There are about 600 students and 25 teachers at Hogwarts. They have classes in the morning and in the afternoon. On Monday and Wednesday mornings they have herbology and potions classes. On Monday and Wednesday afternoons they have quidditch practice (his favorite days) and history of magic on Tuesdays and Thursdays. On Fridays, they have astronomy and defense against the dark arts in the morning, but they don't have classes in the afternoon. Friday afternoons are free. In the evening, they study and socialize. On the weekends they play sports, have fun and rest! Hogwarts is a fantastic school.

	Monday	Tuesday	Wednesday	Thursday	Friday	Saturday	Sunday
MORNING A.M.	herbology potions	transfiguration charms	herbology ______	transfiguration charms	______ defense...	sports have fun rest	sports have fun rest
AFTERNOON P.M.	______	______	______	______	free		
EVENING P.M.	study socialize	study socialize	study socialize	study socialize	study socialize		

GO GET IT

verb to have (neg.) & prepositions of time: on & in

Tip
In English, we write the days of the week with capital letters: Sunday, Monday, Tuesday...

2 **Read the sentences. Look at the Language Login. Check (✓) the correct option.**

1 Harry and his friends don't have quidditch practice on Tuesdays.
◯ affirmative ◯ negative

2 They have astronomy on Fridays.
◯ affirmative ◯ negative

3 Use **in** with...
◯ periods of the day ◯ days of the week

4 Use **on** with...
◯ periods of the day ◯ days of the week

LANGUAGE LOGIN

Verb to have (aff. & neg.) / Prepositions: on & in

I / you / we / they **have**	Math	**on**	Monday mornings.
I / you / we / they **don't have**	Geography		Tuesday afternoons.
	Science		Fridays.
	Portuguese		Thursdays.
		in	the morning.
			the evening.

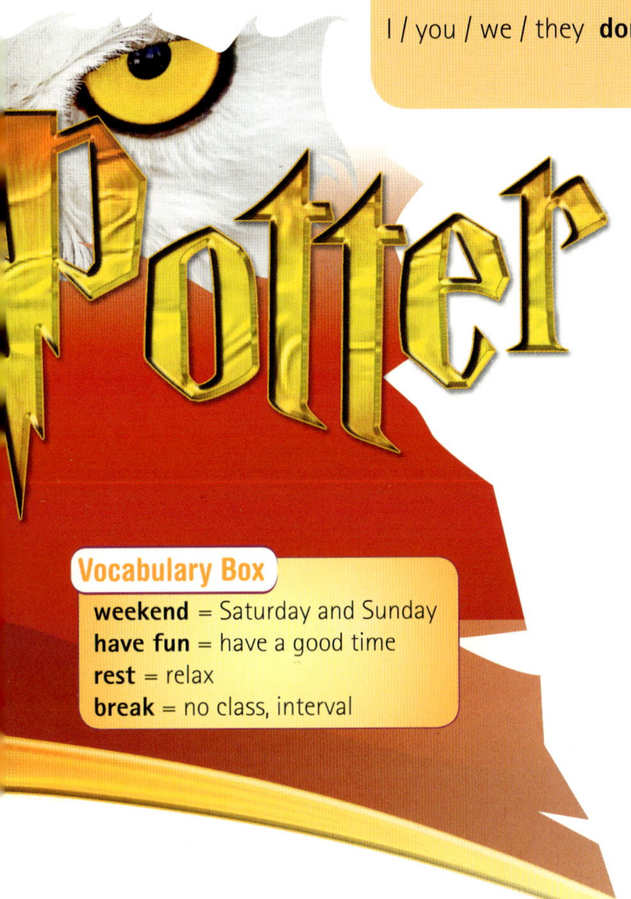

Vocabulary Box

weekend = Saturday and Sunday
have fun = have a good time
rest = relax
break = no class, interval

PRACTICE

3 **Write true sentences about Harry Potter. Use *have* or *don't have.***

1 Harry and his friends ________________ charms in the afternoon.

2 Hogwarts students ________________ history of magic on Tuesdays and Thursdays.

3 They ________________ potions on Tuesdays.

4 **Unscramble the words and write sentences.**

1 Monday / I / History / mornings / on / have / .
I have history on Monday mornings.

2 don't / I / Portuguese / on / have / Tuesday / mornings / .
____

3 We / classes / Saturdays / have / on / don't / .
____

4 English / They / classes / Wednesdays / on / and / have / Mondays / .
____

5 **Look at the school subjects in #2, on pages 58 and 59. Complete the chart with YOUR school schedule.**

I study
◯ in the morning.
◯ in the afternoon.

Mon	Tue	Wed	Thu	Fri	Sat

LOG IN

6 **Writing.**
Look at your schedule in #5. In your notebook, write a paragraph about YOUR school routine.
Example: I have history on Monday mornings. I don't have...

READING & COMPREHENSION

1 **Calvin isn't at school now. He's at home. What's the special time Calvin's father is talking about? Read the cartoon and check (✓) the correct answer.**

◯ It's 2 o'clock. ◯ It's bath time. ◯ It's bed time.

2 **What's Calvin's opinion about baths? Choose an option to complete the last speech bubble in the cartoon.**

◯ I love baths! ◯ I hate baths! ◯ I don't like baths.

GO GET IT

telling the time

3 **What time is it? Look at the Language Login. Match the columns.**

1. It's nine thirty a.m.
2. It's four o'clock.
3. It's ten forty-five p.m.
4. It's seven fifteen a.m.
5. It's noon.
6. It's eight (oh) five a.m.

Look at YOUR watch. What time is it now?

____

Vocabulary Box

12:00 = noon / midday **12:00** = midnight

a.m. = from midnight to noon
p.m. = from noon to midnight

clock =  **watch** = 

10:05 → we write ten five, but we say "ten (oh) five".

LANGUAGE LOGIN

Asking & telling the time

What time is it?

It's 3:30 = It's three thirty.
It's 1:00 = It's one o'clock.
It's 2:45 = It's two forty-five.
It's 5:15 = It's five fifteen.

Prepositions of time: at & from - to

I have history **at** 2 o'clock.
His classes are **from** 7:30 a.m. **to** 3:15 p.m.
Our break is **from** 10:36 **to** 10:50 a.m.

Question word: when

When is your bed time? → It's at 10:00 p.m.
When is the science test? → On Tuesday.

4 **Look at the pictures and answer: What time is it?**

It's two ____________

____

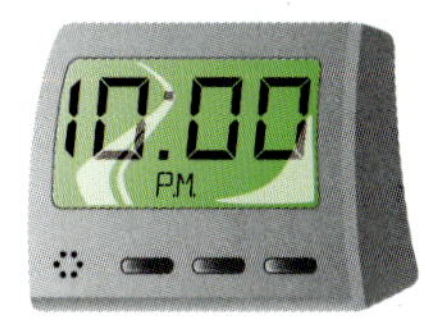

____

LISTENING & PRACTICE

5 **Listen to Calvin's daily routine. Check (✓) the correct time.**

32

When is his...

time for school?	✓ from 7:30 a.m. to 3:15 p.m.	◯ from 7:00 a.m. to 4:15 p.m.
homework time?	◯ from 4 to 4:30 p.m.	◯ at 4 o'clock.
play time?	◯ from 5 to 6:30 a.m.	◯ from 5 to 6:30 p.m.
bath time?	◯ at 6:30 p.m.	◯ at 4:30 p.m.
bed time?	◯ at 10:00 o'clock.	◯ at 9:30 p.m.

6 **Now answer the questions about YOU.**

1 When is your time for school?

____

2 What's your favorite class?

____

3 What's your favorite time of the day?

____

4 What time are your English classes?

____

LOG IN

7 **Practice with a classmate.**
Ask and answer questions about YOUR daily routine.
Use #6 as model.
Add more questions.

Lesson 4

READING

1 **Look at the pictures. Check (✓) the correct options.**

These pictures illustrate bullying. Bullying is a [1] ◯ **good** ◯ **bad** thing. There are bullies everywhere: at school, on the school bus, at the mall...
Bullies [2] ◯ **like** ◯ **don't like** to help people. They are [3] ◯ **rude** ◯ **nice** people. Bullies [4] ◯ **are** ◯ **aren't** friends.

READING & COMPREHENSION

2 **It's early in the morning. Brian and Karen are in the classroom. The teacher isn't there. Read their dialogue and do the exercises.**

33

Brian	Hi, little Barbie. Pink backpack! What about your pencil case? Is it pink too?
Karen	Stop it! I'm not a Barbie! I hate it when you call me Barbie!
Brian	All right, all right! Sorry!
Karen	No problem. But stop bullying me, please!
Brian	OK, Barbie. Go call the teacher!
Karen	You know the teacher is in the teacher's lounge, on the second floor. You're cruel! I don't like you!
Brian	I don't care!

Write T for *true* and F for *false*.

1 [ ] Karen likes pink.
2 [ ] Karen and Brian are good friends.
3 [ ] Karen likes Brian.
4 [ ] Brian is a bully.

Where's the teacher?

____

____

Vocabulary Box

Apologizing and accepting apologies

Sorry! — No problem! / That's all right!

Chunk

I don't care! = It makes no difference to me.

LANGUAGE LOGIN

Prepositions: in, on & at

We use the prepositions **in**, **on** & **at** when we talk about places and with time expressions. Look at the language chunks.

Place

at school	**in** the classroom	**on** the bus
at home	**in** the car	**on** the second floor
at the mall		
at work		

Time

at 7:30	**in** September	**on** Monday
at night	**in** the afternoon	**on** Wednesday morning

GO GET IT

in, on & at

3 **Look at the Language Login. Place the words below under the correct preposition.**

the cafeteria	the library	the morning
the taxi	Saturday	the first floor
July	the movies	2 o'clock

in	on	at
______	______	______
______	______	______
______	______	______
______	______	______

PRACTICE

4 **Choose language chunks from each column in #3 and write sentences.**

1 ______________________________
____

2 ______________________________
____

3 ______________________________
____

5 **Andrew is Brian's classmate. Read his report about his school. Complete with *in*, *on* or *at*.**

I like my school and my favorite subject is science. I have science classes [1] ______ Monday mornings. My science teacher is Mr. Thompson. I think he's cool. I don't like some boys [2] ______ school. They're horrible bullies. Brian is one of them. When he is [3] ______ the classroom, I get scared. I don't like Brian and his friends.

LOG IN

6 **Writing.**
Write a similar report about your school.
Are there bullies in YOUR class or school?

Want more?
Go to Grammar Log - G10 & G11 (p. 94)

Review

1 Puzzle. Read the text and guess the day.

On this day I don't have math in the morning. I don't have science. I don't have English in the afternoon. I don't have history in the afternoon. I have arts, but I don't have PE. What day is it?

____

	MON	TUE	WED	THU	FRI
a.m.	math	history	history	geography	math
	arts	arts	English	science	history
p.m.	history	maths	PE	English	PE
	science	geography	math	arts	science

2 Complete with the prepositions *in*, *on* or *at*.

1 I have science ________ Friday afternoons.
2 My Portuguese class is ________ 3:30.
3 My playmates are ________ the classroom.
4 My birthday is ________ September.
5 Maria's school library is ________ the second floor.
6 I don't have English ________ the mornings.
7 I have tennis classes ________ Mondays.

3 Ask questions for these answers. Use *Where*, *When*, *Who* or *What time*. Then match the questions to the answers.

1 ____What____ is your English teacher's name? [ ] My dad is.
2 ______________ is in the taxi? [ ] In May.
3 ______________ is the library? [ ] At 9:00.
4 ______________ is your arts class? [ ] Mrs. Abbot.
5 ______________ is your birthday? [ ] On the first floor, next to the cafeteria.

4 Unscramble the sentences.

1 My / 8:30 p.m. / bed time / is / at / brother's / .

____

2 like / I / geography / don't / .

____

3 Thursday / I / on / history / afternoons / have / .

____

4 3:00 / school / 3:20 p.m. / break / is / from / My / to / .

____

5 are / bullies / some / my / at / There / school / .

____

5 Complete the crosswords.

1 a school subject
2 a day of the week
3 ________________, afternoon, evening
4 2:15 = It's two ________________.
5 "________________" "No problem."
6 49 – 36 = ________________.
7 Your mother's sister is your ________________.

6 Kevin and Jason are brothers. Number their dialogue in order.

[5] I don't care.
[ ] Excuse me. You're not ugly. You're weird!
[1] Hello, ugly little brother!
[ ] Weird? Me? You're weird!
[ ] Stop it! I'm not ugly!

Is there bullying only at school?

____

7 Write sentences using the prompts given. Add any necessary words.

1 When / have / PE / ?

____

2 I / Spanish classes / Mondays /.

____

3 My brother's / play time / 4:00 to 5:30 p.m. /.

____

4 Mrs. Earp / English teacher / short and funny / .

____

Want more?
Go to Word Log - Unit 6 (p. 100)

Unit 7

Out & about

READING & COMPREHENSION

Lesson 1

1 34 **Dana's an Australian girl. This is her homework: a composition about her everyday activities. Read it and complete the sentences about Dana.**

A DAY IN THE LIFE OF AN AUSTRALIAN TEENAGER

My name's Dana and I'm from Australia. This is a typical day in my life.

I (1) get up at 7 a.m., (2) get dressed for school and have breakfast. I go to school at 8:30. I (3) have lunch at noon. In the afternoon, I play baseball with my friends at school (that's my favorite sport) and then I get home at 5 p.m. When I get home I (4) take a shower and do my homework at 6:15.

I have dinner at 7. After dinner I watch TV. I (5) go to bed at 10:30 p.m. but before that I (6) brush my teeth.

1 Dana is ______________________ .

2 Dana and her friends play baseball after ______________________ .

3 Dana and her family have dinner at ______________________ .

Vocabulary Box

Meals

We have **breakfast** in the morning.
We have **lunch** in the afternoon.
We have **dinner** in the evening.

GO GET IT

pres. simple (aff.)

2 **Look at the Language Login. Read the sentences. Check (✓) the correct option.**

1 ◯ We use the present simple to talk about the time.

2 ◯ We use the present simple to talk about routines.

LANGUAGE LOGIN

Present simple (aff.)

		at 7 o'clock.
I	**watch TV**	at 7:30 every day.
You	**play baseball**	with our best friend.
We	**go to school**	at 6 p.m.
They	**have lunch**	after school.
		at 12:30 p.m.

VOCABULARY WORK

everyday activities

3 **Match the numbers in Dana's composition in #1 with the corresponding pictures.**

PRACTICE

4 **Use the words / expressions from the three columns to make FOUR sentences.**

I	**go to school**	**every day.**
You	**go to bed**	**after school.**
We	**do (my/your/our/their) homework**	**at 7 a.m.**
They	**play soccer**	**on Tuesdays.**
	have lunch	**in the evening.**
	have dinner	**with my friends.**
	have breakfast	**on the weekend.**
	get up	

1 ______________________________

2 ______________________________

3 ______________________________

4 ______________________________

5 **In your notebook, write TWO sentences about YOU. Use the every day activities in orange in #1.**

VOCABULARY WORK

sports & activities

1 **Look at the pictures. Check (✓) the sports and activities YOU like.**

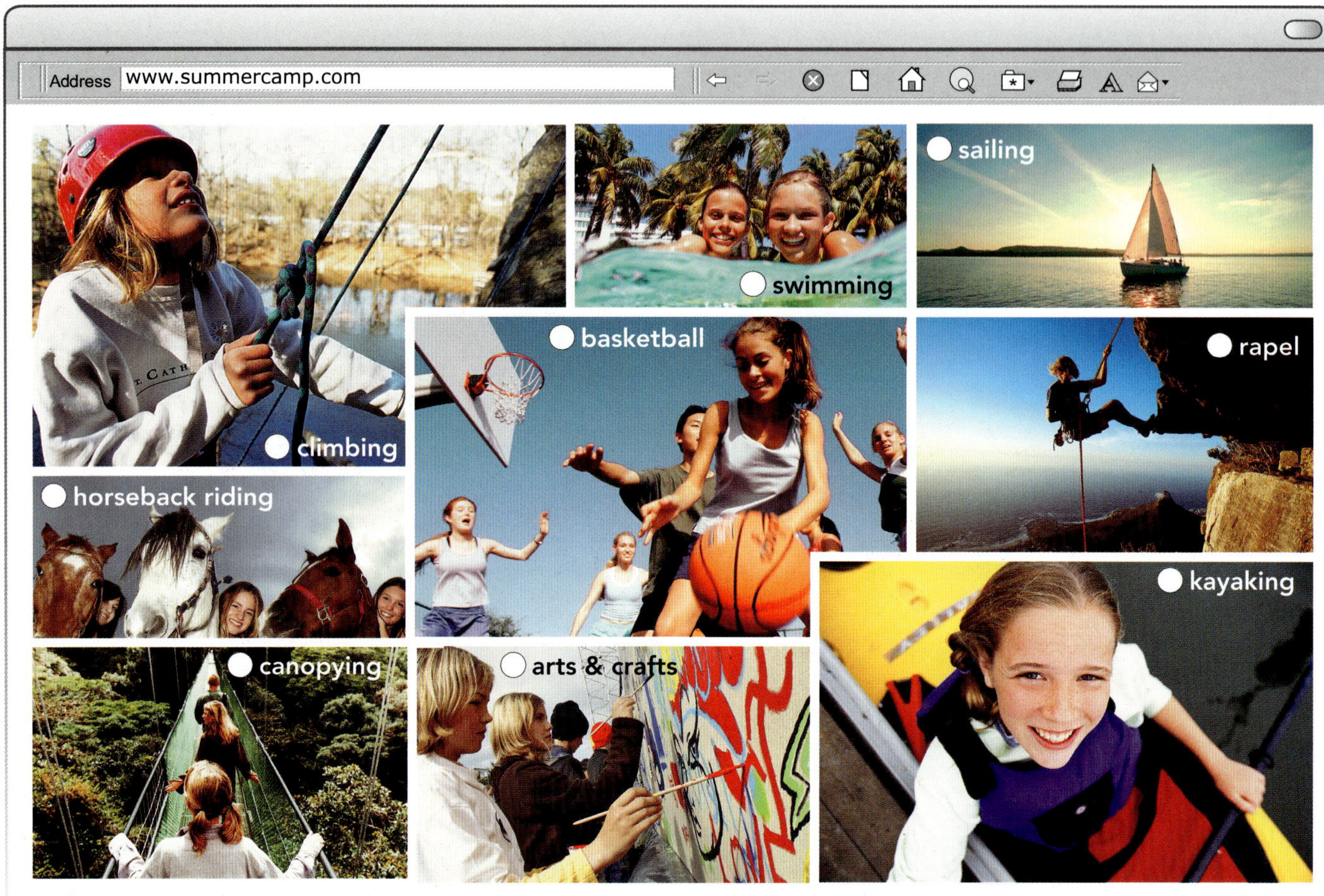

READING & COMPREHENSION

2 **Read this brochure about Green Hills Summer Camp. Then check (✓) the best title.**

35

Green Hills Summer Camp
Suring, Wisconsin

Green Hills Summer Camp is located in the Nicolet National Forest in Wisconsin. We have excellent facilities for boys and girls between 10 and 16: comfortable dormitories, a big cafeteria, a cybercafé, playing fields, an auditorium and a health office. Activities include water sports (swimming, sailing and kayaking), soccer, arts & crafts, horseback riding, climbing and more!

Get in touch with us.

(Adapted from http://camppage.com)

- ◯ Wisconsin: a fantastic place!
- ◯ The perfect summer camp for you!
- ◯ Sports and activities!

3 **Write T for *true* and F for *false*.**

1 [ ] This summer camp is only for boys.
2 [ ] There are no computers in the summer camp.
3 [ ] There are different water sports there.

LANGUAGE LOGIN

Sequencers: first, then, after that

First, I make my bed.
Then, I have breakfast.
After that, I go water skiing and scuba diving.

Attention! Use **first**, **then**, **after that** to organize your ideas in chronological order.

GO GET IT

sequencers

4 Joshua is at Green Hills Summer Camp. Read his schedule, look at Language Login and number the sentences.

[ ] Then, we go horseback riding in the afternoon.
[ ] At noon, we cook and have lunch. It's fun!
[ ] After that, we go climbing.
[1] First, I make my bed.
[ ] Then I'm really tired! I sit down and play computer games.

PRACTICE

5 Read Joshua's e-mail to his friend Paul. Complete the text using *first*, *then* and *after that*.

Folders
Inbox
Friends
Spam
Trash
Sent Mail

Hi, Paul,

Here I am at Green Hills Summer Camp. It's great, man! The place is awesome and we have so many things to do here!
My days are really busy! I get up at 7.

[1] ______________, I make my bed and clean our dormitory.

[2] ______________ I have breakfast and go kayaking on the lake.
We all help with the cooking at about midday. [3] ______________ we go horseback riding and climbing.

[4] ______________ I play computer games.

See you!
Joshua

6 Imagine YOU are at Green Hills Summer Camp. Look at #1. Choose some activities and complete this e-mail to a friend.

First I ______________________________.
Then ______________________________.
After lunch, my friends and I ______________________________
______________________________.
After that ______________________________
______________________________.

READING & COMPREHENSION

1 **Dora and Tom are friends. They chat on MSN every evening. Read their chat. Then match the highlighted words to their meanings.**

36

Dora	U there?
TOM	Yeah. WU?
Dora	Do you have extracurricular classes on Tuesdays?
TOM	Yes. Soccer n drama club. WAY?
Dora	Me 2. Let's go together.
TOM	How do you go 2 school?
Dora	By bus. U?
TOM	By bike.
Dora	Let's go by bike on Tuesday then.
TOM	OK.
Dora	G2B now.
TOM	CY.

1 U	[ ] Me too.
2 WU?	[ ] See you.
3 n	[ ] to
4 WAY?	[ ] Going to bed.
5 Me 2	[ ] and
6 2	[1] You
7 G2B	[ ] What's up?
8 CY	[ ] What about you?

GO GET IT

pres. simple (int.)

2 **Look at the affirmative and interrogative sentences below. What's different?**

1 You have extracurricular classes on Tuesdays.
2 Do you have extracurricular classes on Tuesdays?

3 **Look at the Language Login. Use the words below to write questions for these short anwers.**

1 you / go to school / by car
Do you go to school by car?
Yes, I do.

2 Dora and Tom / go / drama club / ?
____
Yes, they do.

3 they / talk on MSN / every day / ?
____
Yes, they do. In the evening.

4 you / have breakfast / at 7 o'clock / ?
____
No, I don't. I have breakfast at 6:30.

5 they / get up / at 6:30 / ?
____
No, they don't. They get up at 7:30.

Vocabulary Box

How do you go to school?
By bus / car / taxi.
On foot.

LANGUAGE LOGIN

Present simple (int.) & short answers

Do	I	**get up**	at 7 o'clock**?**	Yes, you do. / No, you don't.
	you	**have**	breakfast at 7:30 every day**?**	Yes, I do. / No, I don't.
	we	**have**	PE on Monday**?**	Yes, we do. / No, we don't.
	they	**go**	to school by bus**?**	Yes, they do. / No, they don't.

Attention! We use the auxiliary **DO** before the subject to ask questions using I, you, we and they.

PRACTICE

4 **Look at Harry Potter's schedule on page 60. What are Harry's short answers to these questions?**

1 Do you have herbology on Tuesday mornings?
No, I don't.
____

2 Do you play quidditch on Wednesday afternoons?
____

3 Do you have history of magic on Thursdays?
____

4 Do you have classes on Saturdays?
____

5 **Complete the exercise. Write questions for the answers given or give YOUR short answers.**

1 Do you play tennis?
____

2 _______________?
No, I don't. I get up at 6 a.m.

3 _______________?
Yes, we do. We have dinner at this time every evening.

4 Do you go to school on foot?
____

5 _______________?
No, I don't. I talk on MSN only on the weekends.

6 **Dora and Tom are going home after the drama club. Complete their conversation.**

Tom [1] _______________ you play sports on the weekends?
Dora Yes, I [2] _______________ .
Tom [3] _______________ you [4] _______________ basketball?
Dora No, [5] _______________ .
Tom [6] _______________ [7] _______________ play tennis?
Dora Yeah. I love it!
Tom Let's play together next Saturday.
Dora Great idea!

LOG IN

7 **Practice with a classmate.**
Interview a friend. Use some of the questions from this lesson and create others.

READING

1 **Answer the quiz from a teen magazine.**

TEEN TEST

Do you have a pet?

- ○ a dog
- ○ a cat
- ○ a fish
- ○ a bird
- ○ a hamster
- ○ a parrot
- ? ______

What's your favorite school subject?

- ○ Math
- ○ Arts
- ○ Geography
- ○ History
- ○ PE
- ? ______

Do you have a collection?

- ○ magazines
- ○ stamps
- ○ stuffed animals
- ○ posters
- ○ DVDs
- ○ comic books
- ○ stickers
- ? ______

What do you do in your free time?

- ○ play computer games
- ○ read books
- ○ chat online
- ○ watch TV
- ○ talk to friends
- ○ go surfing
- ? ______

Do you like...

your city?	○ yes	○ no
your neighborhood?	○ yes	○ no
your home?	○ yes	○ no
your room?	○ yes	○ no

Vocabulary Box
home = house or apartment

2 **Use the information from #1 to write about YOU.**

1 In my free time I ______
2 I ○ have ○ don't have a collection. I collect ______
3 I ○ have ○ don't have a pet. It's a ______
4 My favorite school subject is ______
5 I ______ my city.

GO GET IT

pres. simple (neg.)

3 **Vivian has the quiz. She's always in a bad mood. All her answers are negative. Look at the Language Login and complete her sentences.**

LANGUAGE LOGIN

Present simple (neg.)

I	**don't have**	a collection.
You	**don't like**	pets.
We	**don't go**	to school in the morning.
They	**don't get up**	at 7 o'clock.

1 I _don't collect_ (collect) stickers.
2 I ______________ (chat) on line.
3 I ______________ (play) computer games.
4 I ______________ (like) my neighborhood.
5 I ______________ (have) a pet.

PRACTICE

4 **Read the phrases below. Write them in the appropriate box.**

- read magazines
- collect comic books
- have a favorite subject
- make my bed
- play outdoor sports
- help at home
- go to bed late
- watch TV
- listen to music
- have lunch with my family
- get up early
- do homework
- like dogs

Things I do

____

Things I don't do

____

5 **Now choose TWO items from each column in #4 and write sentences about YOU in your notebook.**

Example: *I have lunch with my family. / I don't have lunch with my family.*

LOG IN

6 **Writing.**

Write a quiz to find out the things YOUR friends do or don't do. Use #1 and the phrases from #4 as prompts. Quiz your friends.

1 **Read Piero's letter to Martin. Find and circle FOUR mistakes he made.**

Hi, Martin,

My name Piero. This is his family.
My father and my mother are doctors.
They gets up at 6 o'clock every day.
My sister's name is Priscilla. We get up at 7.
Then we don't go to school.
We like our school. After school I plays
video games.
What about you?

Write soon,
Piero

2 **Go back to #1. Write the sentences correctly.**

Example: My name's Piero.

1 ______________________________

2 ______________________________

3 ______________________________

4 ______________________________

3 **Unscramble the words and make questions.**

1 go to bed / every / do / late / day / you / ?

______________________ → ______________________

2 cycling / go / you / do / Sundays / on / ?

______________________ → ______________________

3 collect / you / do / stuffed animals / ?

______________________ → ______________________

4 you / dinner / after / do / 8 p.m. / have / ?

______________________ → ______________________

4 **Go back to #3 and answer the questions about YOU. Give short answers.**

5 **Complete using *by*, *on*, *at*, or *in*.**

1 My sister and I don't go to school ____ bus.
2 My friends and I play soccer ____ Sunday mornings.
3 Tom and his brother are athletes. They get up ____ 5:00 a.m. every day!
4 My cousins don't have English lessons ____ the mornings.
5 My house is next to my school. I go to school ____ foot.

6 **Look at the pictures and unscramble the words.**

1 ____________________

2 ____________________

3 ____________________

4 ____________________

5 ____________________

6 ____________________

Want more?
Go to Word Log - Unit 7 (p. 100)

7 **Write TWO affirmative and TWO negative sentences about YOU. Use the actions from #6.**

1 ____________________
2 ____________________
3 ____________________
4 ____________________

Unit 8

World magazine flashes

Lesson 1

READING & COMPREHENSION

1 (37) **Read the fact file about Patricia taken from *Future Stars* magazine. Complete the text. Then listen and check.**

FUTURE STARS

Does Patricia Costas have a bright future?

Patricia Costas is a [1] ________ -year-old teenager from [2] ________________ . She's an exchange student in the city of Huntington Beach in California, USA. She studies English every day from 9 a.m. to 2 p.m.

She hates [3] ________________ . On weekends she goes surfing in the morning (she loves it!) and then she goes shopping, plays volleyball and hangs out with her friends.

After school she has lunch and then she has surfing classes. Her teacher, Mark Davis, says she's great and has the talent to be a champion. Mark guarantees: Patricia has a bright future ahead of her. She's a star!

FACT FILE

Name: Patricia Costas
Age: 14
Comes from: Caracas, Venezuela
Loves: shopping, surfing and hanging out with her friends.
Hates: cold days

LANGUAGE LOGIN

Present simple (aff.): 3rd person sing.

Patricia **has** surfing lessons every day.
Mark **teaches** surfing in Huntington Beach.
She **goes** to the mall on weekends.
He **thinks** Patricia's great.

Attention! For the 3rd person singular, we add **s**, **es** or **ies** to the verb.

2 **Check (✓) the correct option.**

1 Patricia studies in ◯ **Caracas** ◯ **the USA**.
2 Patricia loves ◯ **cold days** ◯ **surfing**.
3 Mark Davis thinks she's a ◯ **good** ◯ **bad** surfer.
4 Patricia goes surfing ◯ **from Monday to Friday** ◯ **every day**.

GO GET IT

pres. simple (aff. / 3rd person)

3 **Compare the sentences. What changes from the first to the second column? Underline the differences.**

1 I have a bright future.	Patricia has a bright future.
2 They hate cold days.	She hates cold days.
3 We teach surfing.	He teaches surfing.

Tip
Spelling
think + **s** = think**s**
go + **es** = go**es**
study – y + **ies** = stud**ies**
have – ve + **s** = ha**s**

4 **Look at the Language Login. Complete the sentences.**

1 Patricia's dad ________________ (have) a car.
2 He ________________ (get up) at 6 a.m.
3 Pat ________________ (study) English.
4 She ________________ (love) surfing.

PRACTICE

5 **Read the text Patricia wrote about her favorite female surfer. Complete it with the correct form of the verbs in the box.**

play (2x) | train | work | go (2x) | have (2x) | like | live

Chelsea Elizabeth Hedges is a famous surfer (#1 in 2005!). She competes in the ASP (Association of Surfing Professionals). She's from Sydney, Australia.
She [1] ___has___ two brothers. Her dad [2] ____________ in Avalon and her mom [3] ____________ in a clothing boutique.
Chelsea [4] ____________ dogs, she [5] ____________ a Rottweiler.
She [6] ____________ a lot. On weekends she [7] ____________ golf and [8] ____________ to the movies.
She also [9] ____________ shopping and [10] ____________ tennis.
I think she's fantastic!

(Based on: www.aspworldtour.com)

6 **In your notebook write about YOUR family and friends.**

Example: My mother always cooks lunch on Saturdays.

Lesson 2

READING & COMPREHENSION

1 Read this section of the ***Pet World Magazine***. Match the descriptions with the pictures.

38

Tip
Never buy illegal animals.
It's a crime!
Check: www.ibama.gov.br.

Pet World

Do you have a strange pet?
Send us a picture and a description!

I have a pet spider. Her name's Lola. She's a tarantula. She's quiet and interesting to watch. She has long legs and some hair on her body. She lives in a box. She likes to climb. She eats small insects. Spiders are sometimes dangerous, but Lola is friendly.
(Javier – Mexico)

1

Meet Bella. She's my pet. She's a macaw. She has green feathers and a black and white beak. She has wings. She eats vegetables and fruit. She lives in a cage. Bella is intelligent and funny. She likes to talk to me when I'm home.
(Maria – Lima)

2

3

4

I have a small gecko. His name's Billy. He's yellow and white with black spots. He has short legs and a long tail. He eats insects. He lives in a tank. He doesn't like the day.
(Stephanie – New York)

This is my pet. His name's Buddy. He's black and brown and his fur is soft. He likes to play and sleep. He eats cat food. He's cute and friendly. He's a ferret.
(Aryel – the USA)

80 81

2 Look at the colored phrases in #1. Complete the table.

Pet	Name	Description	Lives in	Eats	Likes	Owner's opinion
A ferret	Buddy	black and brown soft fur	ø	cat food	to play and sleep	cute and friendly
A gecko	________	________ and ________ with black spots	a tank	________	the night	ø
A spider	Lola	________ and ________ on her body	________	small insects	________	quiet, interesting to watch, sometimes dangerous, friendly
A macaw	________	green feathers and a black and white beak	________	vegetables and fruit	to talk	________ and ________

LANGUAGE LOGIN

Present simple: int. & short answers (3rd person sing.)

Affirmative		Interrogative		Short answers
He She It	like**s** to play. eat**s** fruit. live**s** in a box. ha**s** a tail.	**Does he** **Does she** **Does it**	**like** to play? **eat** fruit? **live** in a box? **have** a tail?	**Yes**, he / she / it **does**. **No**, he / she / it **doesn't**.

Vocabulary Box

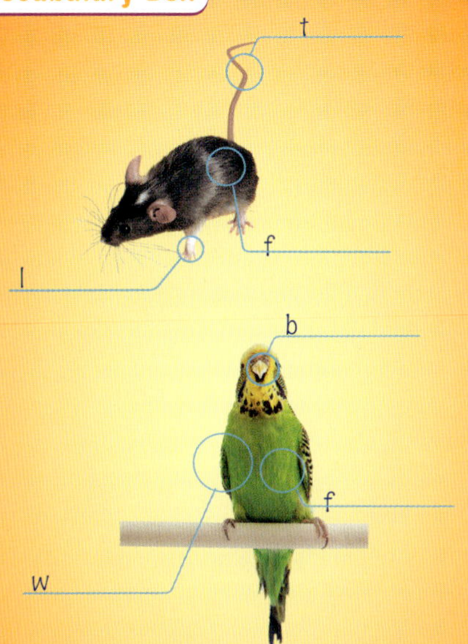

An animal = it
A spider has 8 legs. It eats insects.

A pet you know = he / she
I have a cat. She is white.

GO GET IT

pres. simple (int. / 3rd person sing.)

3 Look at the Language Login. Use the words below to write questions. Answer them with short answers.

1 Aryel / have / ferret / ?
Does Aryel have a ferret?
Yes, she does.

2 Javier's spider / eat / vegetables / ?
____
____
____

3 the macaw / live / in a cage / ?
____
____
____

4 Maria / have / leopard gecko / ?
____
____
____

5 Javier / like / spiders / ?
____
____
____

PRACTICE

4 Write questions for the answers given or give YOUR short answers.

1 Does your best friend have a pet?
____

2 _______________?
No, it doesn't. It only eats cat food.

3 _______________?
Yes, he does. Aryel's ferret loves to play and sleep.

4 Does your school have insect tanks?
____

5 Choose one of the pets on page 80. Ask and answer questions in pairs. Guess which animal it is.

A Does it have a beak?
B No, it doesn't.
A Does it have fur?
B Yes, it does.
A I know! It's a ferret.
B That's right.

READING & COMPREHENSION

1 **Discuss these questions: Do you like pit bulls? Do you think they are dangerous?**

2 **Read this online magazine article showing two different points of view about pit bulls. There's always two sides to a story. What's YOUR opinion?**

39

Search

Join our discussion forum | Post your comments | Pics | Infoweb

Pit Bulls: friends or foes?

There's a lot of controversy around pit bulls. Some people say that these dogs are affectionate and loyal by nature. Some people say that they are dangerous, unpredictable and genetically predisposed to react aggressively.

What do pit bull owners and victims have to say?

DIANE BOURKE has a 2-year-old pit bull called Zorba. Diane says he's a sweet dog. "He loves to be with the family and enjoys playing. He is the guardian of the front door: when the doorbell rings, he barks. But he doesn't bite. On the contrary, he jumps up and down and licks people once they get in. He's easy to train. He doesn't disobey me, and he's so intelligent that he learns new things every day. He doesn't attack other dogs or people. In fact, he's very sociable. Some people find him intimidating, but he doesn't do anything evil or aggressive. He's a great companion. He loves to play in water and enjoys hiking".

GEORGE KING has a different story to tell. "My neighbor, Edward Millet, has a pit bull called Meg. She's 3 years old and is very, very strong. He says she doesn't bite and that she isn't dangerous. He doesn't lock his gate, and very often, Meg escapes and runs freely in the streets. Edward says Meg's friendly so she doesn't wear a muzzle, and he doesn't keep her on a leash! It's the law, but Edward doesn't care. The other day, Meg, 'the sweet dog', attacked my baby son and he was hospitalized. I have no words to express how I feel about it. People like Edward should be in prison".

3 **Complete the sentences according to the online article.**

1 According to Diane, Zorba barks, but he doesn't __________ .

2 Zorba __________ people when they get into Diane's house.

3 According to George, Edward doesn't __________ his gate.

4 Meg doesn't __________ a muzzle.

Vocabulary Box

Find the meaning of the words below with the help of your teacher or dictionary.

bark: __________

bite: __________

lick: __________

a muzzle: __________

a leash: __________

GO GET IT

pres. simple (neg. / 3rd person sing.)

4 **Look at the Language Login. Go back to the article in #2 and find THREE other sentences in the negative form. Copy them here.**

1 ______________________________

2 ______________________________

3 ______________________________

LANGUAGE LOGIN

Present simple (neg.) – 3rd person sing.

He	**doesn't keep**	the dog on a leash.
She	**doesn't think**	pit bulls are dangerous.
It	**doesn't wear**	a muzzle.

PRACTICE

5 **There's a mistake in each sentence. Circle it and rewrite the sentences correctly in your notebook.**

1 Daniel don't have a pit bull. His dog is a labrador.
2 Christine take doesn't her dog for a walk.
3 Zoe doesn't likes dogs. She has a cat.
4 My dog don't barks a lot.

6 **Use the elements below to make FIVE sentences. Practice all the forms: affirmative, negative and interrogative. Write them in your notebook.**

Example: *She doesn't brush her teeth after lunch.*

I you we they he she it

LOG IN

7 **Practice with a classmate.**
Are YOU a cat or a dog person?
Imagine you have a cat or a dog. Prepare arguments in favor of your pet. Use ideas and the highlighted adjectives from the online article in #2 to help you. Try to convince your friend.

Want more?
Go to Grammar Log - G12 (p. 95)

Lesson 4

VOCABULARY WORK

adjectives

1 **With the help of your teacher or a dictionary, check the meaning of the highlighted words in #2.**

READING & COMPREHENSION

2 **Read this magazine article about Chinese horoscopes. Which animal are YOU? Is your personality description correct?**

40

Dragon
Dragons help their friends. They are courageous but sometimes they are eccentric.

Snake
Snakes are very instinctive. They believe in intuition. They are determined and love success.

FIND YOUR CHINESE SIGN:

Rat	1984	1996
Ox	1985	1997
Tiger	1986	1998
Rabbit	1987	1999
Dragon	1988	2000
Snake	1989	2001
Horse	1990	2002
Sheep	1991	2003
Monkey	1992	2004
Rooster	1993	2005
Dog	1994	2006
Pig	1995	2007

Horse
Horses have a lot of energy and love adventure. They are popular but sometimes very impatient.

Sheep
Sheep like beauty and the arts. They like their friends but are shy with others.

Monkey
Monkeys are very social. They love parties! They are creative and intelligent and like to solve problems.

Rooster
Roosters are practical and work hard every day. They like beautiful things. They don't have many friends and they always think they're right. They never listen to other people.

Dog
Dogs are honest and keep their friends' secrets. They are critical and sometimes distant at parties.

Pig
Pigs are intelligent and like to help people. They don't have many friends. They are quiet and like to study.

Rat
Rats like to learn about new things. They're charming, funny and intelligent. They like perfection.

Ox
Oxes are determined and patient. They don't talk much and they are often angry at little things.

Tiger
Tigers are natural leaders. They always fight for what's right. They like to think but sometimes they find it difficult to make a decision.

Rabbit
Rabbits are popular and have many friends. They like to protect people. They don't like conflict.

Vocabulary Box

Saying the years

1999 = **19 99** = nineteen ninety-nine

2000 = two thousand

2003 = two thousand and three

Irregular plurals

One sheep → three sheep

One fish → five fish

LANGUAGE LOGIN

Adverbs of frequency

The adverbs of frequency tell you when something happens.

✓	✓	✓	✓	✓	✓	**Always** → Dragons always help their friends.
✓		✓		✓	✓	**Often** → Monkeys are often creative.
	✓		✓			**Sometimes** → Dogs are sometimes distant at parties.
						Never → Roosters never listen to people.

Attention! Be careful with the position of the adverbs of frequency in relation to the verbs.

An ox is **often** angry. = verb to be + **adverb**
Snakes **often** believe in intuition. = **adverb** + full verb

GO GET IT

adverbs of frequency

3 Look at the Language Login. What do these sentences mean? Check (✓) the correct options

1 I **always** read the horoscope page.
◯ I read it every day. ◯ I don't read it.

2 She **often** reads the horoscope page.
◯ She reads it every day .
◯ She reads it almost every day.

3 He **sometimes** reads the horoscope page.
◯ He doesn't read it. ◯ He reads it some days.

4 We **never** read the horoscope page.
◯ We don't read it. ◯ We read it every day.

PRACTICE

4 Look at the texts in #2. Write the correct *adverb of frequency*.

1 Rabbits __often__ protect people.
2 Roosters ________ work hard.
3 Snakes ________ use their intuition to solve problems.
4 Dogs ________ tell their friends' secrets.

5 Think about the real animals now. Rewrite the sentences adding the *adverbs of frequency*.

1 Snakes are dangerous. (sometimes)
Snakes are sometimes dangerous.

2 Rats don't like cats. (often)

3 Monkeys are very funny. (often)

4 Horses eat meat. (never)

5 Rabbits have long ears. (always)

6 Dogs bite their owners. (sometimes)

Want more?
Go to Grammar Log - G13 (p. 96)

LOG IN

6 Writing.
Think of YOUR best friend. What's his / her Chinese horoscope? Does he / she follow the description in #2? Write his / her profile.

Review

1 **Match the columns. Make possible pairs.**

1 go	[ ] lunch
2 have	[ ] games
3 collect	[ ] in a nice neighborhood
4 read	[1] to school
5 play	[ ] patient
6 chat	[ ] a book
7 eat	[ ] stickers
8 watch	[ ] online
9 live	[ ] vegetables
10 be	[ ] TV

2 **Write sentences using THREE pairs from #1.**

Example: *I go to school in the mornings.*

1 ____________________

2 ____________________

3 ____________________

3 **Write questions for the answers given or give YOUR short answers.**

1 Do you always take a shower in the morning? ____________________

2 ____________________ No, she doesn't. Mary goes to school by bus.

3 ____________________ Yes, sometimes pit bulls attack people.

4 Does your grandmother live near your house? ____________________

5 Do you have a pet? ____________________

4 **Use the words from the three columns below to make sentences. Remember to put the verbs in the correct form and the adverbs of frequency in the correct place.**

I My friend My friends My teacher Peter ________	talk in class listen to the radio do homework have breakfast be funny watch TV go cycling read a book chat on the MSN be angry ________	always often sometimes never

1 *My friend is always funny.*

2 ____________________

3 ____________________

4 ____________________

5 ____________________

5 **Follow the model. Correct the sentences below.**

1 Cats eat vegetables. (cat food)
They don't eat vegetables. They eat cat food.

2 Chelsea Elizabeth Hedges plays soccer on the weekends. (golf)
____

3 Javier has a pit bull. (tarantula)
____

4 Maria's macaw lives in a box. (in a cage)
____

5 Birds have fur. (feathers)
____

6 **Write the names of two animals that...**

1 have a long tail: _______________ and _______________

2 are dangerous: _______________ and _______________

3 eat vegetables: _______________ and _______________

4 have soft fur: _______________ and _______________

7 **How many sentences can you write with these words?**

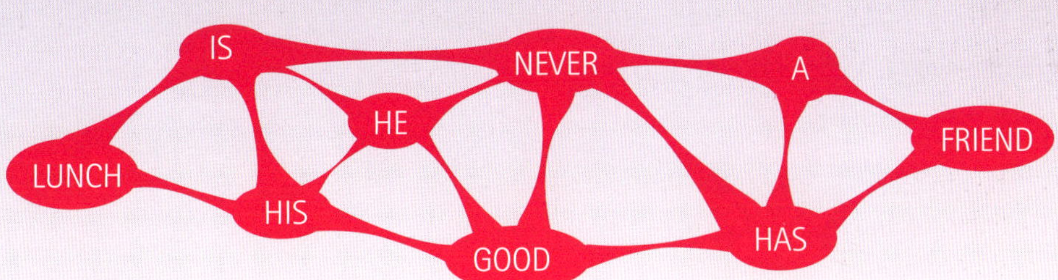

Example: *He is a good friend.*

____

____

____

____

____

Want more?
Go to Word Log - Unit 8 (p. 101)

KEEPING A VOCABULARY LOG

1 **Look at Rebecca's vocabulary notebook.**

2 **What strategies does Rebecca use to keep new vocabulary? Number the examples.**

1 example sentence
2 word combinations
3 illustration
4 explanation
5 translation

3 **Use these strategies to keep a vocabulary notebook. Try different ways of recording vocabulary and choose your favorite ones.**

G1 Question words / Personal information – Preposition / *in* + month

G1
I feel
:-D
:-)
:-/

What	's your name?	My name's Chris.
Where	are you from?	I'm from the USA. I'm American.
How old	are you?	I'm twelve (years old).
When	is your birthday?	My birthday is in May.
How	do you spell your name?	C – H – R – I – S – T – I – N – E

1 **Look at G1 box. Write the questions in the dialogue.**

Lucy [1] ____________________
Dora Dora. Dora Thornycroft.
Lucy [2] ____________________
Dora T – H – O – R – N – Y – C – R – O – F – T.
Lucy [3] ____________________
Dora 13.
Lucy [4] ____________________
Dora In July.
Lucy [5] ____________________
Dora I'm from South Africa.
Lucy OK, Dora. Welcome to our school.

G2 Verb TO BE

G2
I feel
:-D
:-)
:-/

	Affirmative	Negative	Interrogative	Short answers
I	am	am not	Am I...?	Yes, I am. No, I am not.
You / We / They	are	aren't	Are you / we / they...?	Yes, you / we / they are. No, you / we / they aren't.
He / She / It	is	isn't	Is he / she / it...?	Yes, he / she / it is. No, he / she / it isn't.

Grammar log Units 1 & 2

Grammar log Units 2 & 3

1 **Look at G2 box. Check (✓) the correct options.**

1 ☐ isn't = is not
2 ☐ We use **is** with he and they.
3 ☐ **No, I'm not** is a short answer.

2 **Complete the sentences with the correct form of the verb to be.**

1 My father ________ Brazilian. He's Mexican.
2 "________ they from Argentina?" "Yes, they're from Buenos Aires."
3 We ________ good friends.
4 "________ Peter tall or short?" "He's tall."

G3 Subject pronouns & Possessive adjectives

Subject pronouns		Possessive adjectives	
I	'm a singer.	My	eyes are brown.
You	're Brazilian.	Your	mom is Brazilian too.
He	's my friend.	His	eyes are green.
She	's beautiful.	Her	hair is long.
It	's a flag.	Its	colors are green, yellow and blue.
We	're classmates.	Our	class is 2C.
They	're soccer players.	Their	favorite sport is soccer.

G3
I feel
:-D
:-)
:-/

1 **Look at G3 box. Complete the sentences using the correct subjet pronouns and possessive adjectives.**

1 That's not Emily! ________ is slim and ________ eyes are brown.
2 Roger's American. ________ mom is from Mexico and ________ dad is Chilean.
3 Juan and Oscar love soccer. ________ favorite soccer team is Real Madrid. ________ are very good friends.
4 I'm not a sportsperson but ________ love sports. ________ favorite sport is tennis.
5 My classmates and I are very happy. ________ new teacher is really great, and ________ think he's funny.

G4 Demonstrative pronouns & Indefinite articles

G4
I feel
:-D
:-)
:-/

	Demonstrative pronouns		Indefinite articles		
Singular	What's	this?	It's	a	calculator.
		that?		an	eraser.
Plural	What are	these?	They're		Lucas's glasses.
		those?			the boy's glasses.

1 **Look at G4 box. Check (✓) the correct options.**

1 Use ☐ a ☐ **an** before a vowel sound.
2 Use ☐ a ☐ **an** before a consonant sound.
3 Use ☐ **this** ☐ **that** to show an object near you.
4 Use ☐ **these** ☐ **those** to show objects and people that aren't near you.
5 Put ☐ **'s** ☐ **ø** after singular nouns and people's names to indicate possession.

2 **Look at the pictures. Complete the sentences.**

1 ______________'s my mom's umbrella.

2 What are ______________ ?
They're my glasses.

3 ______________ are my roller skates.

4 What's ______________ ?
It's my MP4 player.

G5 There is / There are

G5
I feel
:-D
:-)
:-/

	Affirmative	Negative	Interrogative	Short answers
Singular	There is...	There isn't... There is no...	Is there...?	Yes, there is. No, there isn't.
Plural	There are...	There aren't any... There are no...	Are there any...?	Yes, there are. No, there aren't.

Attention **There isn't** a pen in my backpack. = **There is no** pen in my backpack.
NOT **There is no** ~~a~~ pen in my backpack.

G6 Prepositions of place

G6
I feel
:-D
:-)
:-/

1 Study the G5 and G6 boxes. Look at the picture on page 40. Write true sentences about it.

1 ____________________ a cell phone on the computer.
2 ____________________ CDs on the bed.
3 ____________________ a diary on the bed.
4 ____________________ glasses under the bed.
5 ____________________ a backpack between the desk and the chair.
6 ____________________ sneakers in the bedroom.

G7 Question words

G7
I feel
:-D
:-)
:-/

Where	is my cellphone? are your glasses?	It's next to the computer. They're in my backpack.
How many	books are there?	There are fifteen.

1 Look at G7 box. Choose the correct question word to complete the questions.

1 __________ are the boys?
At the cafeteria.
2 __________ students are there?
Twenty-five, I think.
3 __________ laptops are there?
None.
4 __________ is my diary?
It's under the chair. Look!

G8 Verb TO HAVE

	Affirmative	Negative
I You We They	have...	don't have...

	Affirmative
He She It	has...

1 **Look at G8. Complete with *have* or *has*. Add the necessary information to make true sentences about YOU, your family and friends.**

1 I have ________________ eyes.
2 My best friend ________________ ________________ hair.
3 My parents ________________ ________________ children.
4 My teacher ________________ many students.

Attention **There is** a pen under the chair.
NOT ~~Have~~ a pen under the chair.

G8
I feel
:-D
:-)
:-/

G9 Likes & dislikes

I	love like don't like hate	sports.

Attention **I like** sports.
NOT I ~~am~~ like sports.

G9
I feel
:-D
:-)
:-/

1 **Look at G9. Write true sentences.**

1 I ________________________ PE.
2 I ________________________ swimming.
3 I ________________________ Orlando Bloom.
4 I ________________________ Simple Plan.

Grammar log Units 5 & 6

G10 Prepositions of time & place

time place	on	Monday / Tuesday afternoon the bus / the second floor		
time place	in	the morning / 2009 the classroom / the car		
time place	at	4 o'clock / 5 p.m. school / work / home		
time place	from	Monday Rio de Janeiro	to	Friday Recife

G10
I feel
:-D
:-)
:-/

1 **Study G10 box. Complete the sentences using the verb to have and the correct prepositions of time and place.**

1 I ______________ history ________ Wednesdays.
2 I ______________ tennis lessons ________ the morning.
3 I ______________ classes ________ Saturdays.
4 Victor's brother ______________ many friends ________ school.
5 Leo's classroom is ________ the first floor.
6 Clara's dad is ________ work ________ 9:00 a.m. ________ 7:00 p.m.

G11 Question words

When	is your birthday?	In May.
	do you have English classes?	On Tuesdays and Thursdays.
What time	is it?	It's 7:30.
	do you have English classes?	At 3 o'clock.

G11
I feel
:-D
:-)
:-/

1 **Look at the G10 and G11 boxes. Complete the dialogue.**

Dee ______________________________
Mark It's 2:15.
Dee Let's go! The tennis club is open ________ 2 ________ 5.
Mark Wait a minute! ________ do we have history test?
Dee Oops! ________ 3 o'clock.
Mark So, let's go to school!

G12 Present simple

	Affirmative	Negative	Interrogative			Short answers		
I	play...	don't play.	Do	I	play...?	Yes,	I	do.
You	have...	don't have.		you	have...?		you	
We	like...	don't like.		we	like...?	No,	we	don't.
They				they			they	

Affirmative	
He	plays...
She	has...
It	likes...

Interrogative			Short answers		
Does	he	play...?	Yes,	he	does
	she	have...?		she	
	it	like...?	No,	it	doesn't

G12
I feel
:-D
:-)
:-/

1 **Study the G12 boxes. Complete the sentences with the correct form of the verb in parentheses.**

1 Isabel ______________ (love) surfing.
2 Jane and Jill ______________ (go) to the mall on the weekends.
3 Tom ______________ (study) French on Mondays.
4 My friend ______________ (get up) at 6 a.m. every day.
5 We ______________ (play) soccer on Saturdays.

2 **Give true short answers to the questions below.**

1 Do your parents have a car? ______________________________
2 Do your classmates play soccer? ______________________________
3 Do you have PE on Tuesdays? ______________________________

3 **Use the words below to form questions. Give short answers.**

1 Dina / play volleyball / ?
Does Dina play volleyball? Yes, she does.
2 Peter / like sports / ?
______________________________ No, ______________
3 Jane / get up at 6 a.m. / ?
______________________________ No, ______________
4 Daniel / go to school by car / ?
______________________________ Yes, ______________

Attention
Do you play tennis?
Yes, I do.
NOT Yes, I ~~play.~~

Unit 8 Grammar log

G13 Adverbs of frequency

G13
I feel
:-D
:-)
:-/

Adverbs BEFORE full verbs			
I	always	**help**	people.
My sister	often	**studies**	on weekends.
People	sometimes	**do**	fantastic things!
Paul	never	**eats**	meat.

Adverbs AFTER verb to Be			
I	**am**	always	interested in wildlife.
My sister	**is**	often	happy.
People	**are**	sometimes	afraid of spiders.
Paul	**is**	never	cruel to animals.

1 Look at the G13 boxes. Put the words in order to form sentences.

1 my / is / happy / always / aunt / .

____

2 goes / Sue / to / by / never / school / bus / .

____

3 very / is / rude / he / sometimes / .

____

4 often / soccer / we / on / play / Sundays / .

____

2 Read Kimiko's paragraph about her dog. Underline and correct FOUR mistakes.

Tina is my 2-year-old labrador. She is very friendly so she wears never a muzzle. There is no need for that. Always we go to the park in the afternoon after school. She loves it. We play sometimes with a ball and we often are tired when we get home.

1 ______________________________
2 ______________________________
3 ______________________________
4 ______________________________

WELCOME UNIT

Numbers

One to twenty	p. 5

Classroom objects

a b________	p. 6
a clock	p. 6
a computer	p. 6
a desk	p. 6
a d________	p. 6
an e________	p. 6
a n________	p. 6
a pen	p. 6
a p________	p. 6
a pencil case	p. 6
a wastebasket	p. 6
a whiteboard	p. 6

Saying goodbye

Bye / Goodbye	p. 5
Have to go!	p. 5
See you!	p. 5

Chunks

Can you repeat that, please?	p. 6
How do you spell it?	p. 5
How old are you?	p. 4
I know. / I don't know.	p. 6
I'm in class...	p. 4
I'm (name).	p. 4
I'm... (years old).	p. 4
My last name is...	p. 4
My name's...	p. 4
That's great!	p. 5
What about you?	p. 5
What's your (last) name?	p. 4

Commands

Can I get some ________ ?	p. 7
Close the d________ .	p. 7
Listen to the CD.	p. 7
Look at the ________ .	p. 7
May I go to the ________ ?	p. 7
Open your book.	p. 7
Read the ________ .	p. 7
Write your name.	p. 7

Greetings

Hello / Hi	p. 5

UNIT 1

Countries

A________	p. 9
Australia	p. 11
Brazil	p. 9
C________	p. 9
Chile	p. 16
China	p. 9
F________	p. 9
G________	p. 9
Great Britain	p. 9
Greece	p. 13
I________	p. 9
Japan	p. 9
Mexico	p. 9
Portugal	p. 13
Puerto Rico	p. 13
South Africa	p. 9
the USA	p. 9

Nationalities

American	p. 9
Argentinian	p. 9
Australian	p. 11
Brazilian	p. 9
British	p. 9
Canadian	p. 9
Chinese	p. 9
French	p. 9
German	p. 9
Greek	p. 13
Italian	p. 9
Japanese	p. 9
Mexican	p. 9
Peruvian	p. 13
South African	p. 9

Adjectives

beautiful	p. 13
famous	p. 10
smart	p. 10

Months of the year

January to December	p. 14

Colors

Colors	p. 12

Chunks

He's / she's from...	p. 10
How old is he / she?	p. 11
I'm an avatar.	p. 17
I'm from...	p. 8
I think...	p. 10
It's from...	p. 12
My birthday is in...	p. 14
My e-mail address is...	p. 14
My favorite color is...	p. 17
No, sorry.	p. 16
Thank you.	p. 17
That's right!	p. 16
Try again.	p. 16
What color is...?	p. 13
What's your e-mail address?	p. 14
What's your full name?	p. 8
What's your phone number?	p. 14
When is your birthday?	p. 14
Where are you from?	p. 8
Where's he / she from?	p. 10
Where's it from?	p. 12

UNIT 2

Parts of the body p. 18

Adjectives

- ◯ awesome p. 24
- ◯ bad p. 22
- ◯ beautiful p. 22
- ◯ blond p. 18
- ◯ boring p. 24
- ◯ brave p. 23
- ◯ cool p. 20
- ◯ cute p. 24
- ◯ dark + (color) p. 23
- ◯ fantastic p. 20
- ◯ friendly p. 24
- ◯ funny p. 18
- ◯ good p. 18
- ◯ gorgeous p. 24
- ◯ great p. 20
- ◯ intelligent p. 18
- ◯ interesting p. 18
- ◯ long (hair) p. 26
- ◯ nice p. 24
- ◯ OK p. 24
- ◯ powerful p. 22
- ◯ rude p. 24
- ◯ short p. 22
- ◯ slim p. 22
- ◯ strong p. 18
- ◯ tall p. 18
- ◯ ugly p. 24
- ◯ weird p. 24

Sports p. 20

Interests

- anime p. 18
- computer games p. 18

Country

- England p. 21

Chunks

- Cool! p. 21
- Dear (name), p. 18
- Gee... p. 21
- Get real! p. 21
- Great idea. p. 21
- I agree. / I don't agree. p. 24
- I think it's very interesting! p. 18
- My best friend is... p. 18
- What's your favorite sport? p. 20
- Write soon! p. 18
- Wow! p. 20
- Your e-pal p. 18

Occupations

- an actor p. 24
- an athlete p. 20
- a basketball player p. 21
- a cyclist p. 21
- a gymnast p. 21
- a movie star p. 21
- a singer p. 27
- a skateboarder p. 21
- a soccer player p. 21
- a surfer p. 21
- a swimmer p. 21
- a teacher p. 25
- a tennis player p. 20
- a writer p. 24

Titles

- Mr. / Mrs. / Ms. / Miss p. 25

Nationalities

- Portuguese p. 21
- Russian p. 20

UNIT 3

Classroom objects

- ___ calculator p. 29
- ___ electronic organizer p. 29
- ___ mechanical pencil p. 28

Personal objects

- ___ backpack p. 30
- ___ ball p. 34
- ___ CD p. 33
- ___ cell phone p. 30
- ___ glasses p. 30
- ___ key rings p. 30
- ___ lipstick p. 30
- ___ Matchbox car p. 32
- ___ MP3 player p. 30
- ___ musical instrument p. 35
- ___ poster p. 32
- ___ roller skates p. 32
- ___ sneakers p. 36
- ___ stuffed animals p. 32
- ___ TV p. 33
- ___ umbrella p. 32
- ___ video game p. 33
- ___ wallet p. 30

Chunks

- Can I borrow it / your...? p. 32
- Come on... p. 28
- Easy! p. 28
- Exactly! p. 30
- Go skateboarding. p. 33
- Have a garage sale. p. 33
- Hey, what's up...? p. 30
- I see... p. 30
- Listen to a CD. p. 33
- Money, please! p. 32
- Nothing! p. 30
- No way! p. 32
- Oh, no. Let's do something else! p. 33
- OK. Let me test you now! p. 28
- Oh yeah! p. 28
- Play a computer game. p. 33
- Silly me! p. 28
- Tell me! p. 30
- That's right. p. 29
- Try to remember. p. 28
- Watch TV. p. 33
- Well done! p. 28
- What do you call this in English? p. 28

>>

UNIT 4

Objects

a backpack p. 40
a chair p. 40
a diary p. 40
a stuff p. 40
a window p. 40

Sports

football p. 38
hockey p. 38
ice skating p. 38
soccer p. 38

Extracurricular activities

drama p. 38
foreign languages
(Spanish and French) p. 38
music p. 38

Neighborhood facilities

a cybercafé p. 42
a diner p. 42
a hospital p. 42
a mall p. 38
a movie theater p. 42
a park p. 42
a school p. 42
a store p. 42
a subway station p. 38
a supermarket p. 38
a restaurant p. 42

Chunks

Come in. p. 40
I don't believe it! p. 40
I don't mind. p. 40
I love my neighborhood. p. 46
I miss you all. p. 44
It isn't important to me. p. 41
It's awesome! p. 44
It's horrible! p. 40
It's gross! p. 41
It's right here. p. 40
Let's go! p. 40
My favorite teacher is.... p. 44
That's disgusting! p. 40
We're late. p. 40
What a mess! p. 40
Your point. / My point. p. 47
Write soon! p. 44

School facilities

administrative offices p. 38
an a__________ p. 38
bathrooms p. 38
a c__________ p. 38
classrooms p. 38
a computer lab p. 38
a g________ p. 38
a health office p. 38
l__________ p. 38
a playing field p. 38
a __________ lab p. 38

Numbers

Twenty to fifty p. 44

Adjectives

calm p. 42
fat p. 44
gross p. 41
new p. 44

UNIT 5

Family members

___nt p. 48
br__th__r p. 49
ch__ldr__n p. 48
c___s__ns p. 49
d___ght__r p. 48
f__th__r / d__d / d__ddy p. 48
gr__ndf__th__r p. 48
gr__ndm__th__r p. 49
gr__ndp__r__nts p. 49
h__lf s__st__r p. 48
m__th__r / m__m / m__mmy p. 48
p__r__nts p. 48
s__st__r p. 49
s__ns p. 48
st__pf__th__r p. 48
st__pm__th__r p. 48
twin brother p. 54
__ncl__ p. 49

Parts of the body p. 50

Chunks

I love my mom! p. 54
It's a beautiful afternoon! p. 52
No way! p. 53
Oh no, please! p. 52
She's divorced from... /
married to... p. 48
go to the park p. 53
go on a picnic / have a picnic p. 52
go cycling p. 53
go for a walk p. 53
go bowling p. 53
play + sports p. 53
There's a lot of work. p. 55

Adjectives

adopted p. 48
big p. 48
comfortable p. 48
famous p. 50
happy p. 48
international p. 48
stupid p. 52
ugly p. 51

Countries & nationalities

Cambodian p. 48
Ethiopian p. 48

>>

- Malawi p. 50
- Vietnamese p. 48

Occupations

- an actress / actor p. 50
- an architect p. 54
- a diplomat p. 48
- a director p. 50
- farmers p. 55
- a flight attendant p. 54
- a lawyer p. 54
- a manager p. 54
- a nurse p. 54
- a police officer p. 54
- a sales clerk p. 54
- a secretary p. 54
- a tour guide p. 54
- a web designer p. 54

UNIT 6

School subjects

- A____________ p. 58
- E____________ p. 66
- G____________ p. 58
- H____________ p. 58
- Home ____________ p. 58
- Math / Mathematics p. 58
- ____________ - PE p. 58
- S____________ p. 58

Days of the week

- Monday to Sunday p. 60
- weekend p. 60

Parts of the day

- afternoon p. 61
- a.m. p. 62
- evening p. 61
- midnight p. 62
- morning p. 61
- noon p. 62
- p.m. p. 62

Apologizing & accepting apologies

- No problem. p. 64
- Sorry! p. 64
- That's all right. p. 64

Chunks

- Be a friend. p. 64
- a break p. 61
- Don't be a bully. p. 64
- get scared p. 65
- Have a good time. p. 61
- Have fun. p. 60
- I don't care. p. 64

Asking the time

- What time is it? p. 62
- It's... / It's ... o'clock. p. 62
- time for school p. 63
- homework time p. 63
- play time p. 63
- bath time p. 62
- bed time p. 63

UNIT 7

Meals p. 68

Everyday activities

- brush (one's) ____________ p. 68
- do h____________ p. 68
- get d____________ p. 68
- get h____________ p. 68
- get ____________ (early) p. 68
- go to bed (late) p. 68
- go to s____________ p. 68
- have ____________, lunch, dinner p. 68
- help at h____________ p. 75
- make (one's) ____________ p. 71
- sleep late p. 76
- take a ____________ p. 68
- watch ____________ p. 68

Chunks

- Get in touch with us. p. 70
- How do you go (to school)? p. 72
- See you! p. 71

Collectables

- comic books p. 74
- magazines p. 74
- photos p. 74
- posters p. 74
- stickers p. 74

Pets

- ◯ a bird p. 74
- ◯ a dog p. 74
- ◯ a cat p. 74
- ◯ a fish p. 74
- ◯ a hamster p. 74
- ◯ a parrot p. 74

Sports & activities

- ◯ arts & crafts p. 70
- ◯ baseball p. 68
- ◯ chat online p. 74
- ◯ climbing p. 70
- ◯ canopying p. 70
- ◯ collect things p. 74
- ◯ horseback riding p. 70
- ◯ kayaking p. 70
- ◯ listen to music p. 75
- ◯ rappel p. 70
- ◯ read magazines p. 75
- ◯ sailing p. 70
- ◯ play computer games p. 71

>>

UNIT 8

Adjectives

affectionate p. 82
aggressive p. 82
angry p. 84
courageous p. 84
creative p. 84
critical p. 84
dangerous p. 80
determined p. 84
impatient p. 84
interesting p. 80
intimidating p. 82
loyal p. 82
patient p. 84
popular p. 84
practical p. 84
quiet p. 80
right p. 84
short p. 80
shy p. 84
small p. 80
sociable p. 82
soft p. 80
sweet p. 82
unpredictable p. 82

Verbs

○ attack p. 82
○ bark p. 82
○ bite p. 82
○ come from p. 78
○ hang out p. 78
○ join p. 82
○ jump p. 82
○ keep p. 82
○ lick p. 82
○ live p. 79
○ lock p. 82
○ obey / disobey p. 82
○ post p. 82
○ study p. 78

Nouns

a box p. 80
a cage p. 80
cat food p. 80
front door p. 82
a gate p. 82
horoscope p. 84
insects p. 80
a leash p. 80
meat p. 85
a muzzle p. 82
streets p. 82
a tank p. 80
vegetables and fruit p. 80

Chunks

to be a star p. 78
a bright future p. 78
an exchange student p. 78
What's your side? p. 82

Activities

hanging out with friends p. 78
hiking p. 82
shopping p. 78
surfing p. 78

Animals / pets

a dog p. 84
a dragon p. 84
a gecko p. 80
a horse p. 84
a macaw p. 80
a monkey p. 84
an ox p. 84
a pig p. 84
a rabbit p. 84
a rat p. 84
a rooster p. 84
a sheep p. 84
a snake p. 84
a spider p. 80
a tarantula p. 80
a tiger p. 84

WORLD ISSUES MAGAZINE

WI 1: We are all in this world together!

Sports

WI 2: What's beauty?

Nouns

fairytale
friendship
heart
movie review
ogre
skin

Adjectives

gorgeous
important
weird

WI 3: Friends around the world

Computer related words / phrases
blog
chat on MSN
e-pals
surf the Internet

Chunks
a helping hand
to be down (to be sad)
to be cold (to be distant)

WI 4: The place where we live

Nouns
a city
an industry
a palace
a pool
a university

Chunks
Don't throw trash in the streets.
Don't waste paper.
Keep the city clean.
Protect parks and trees.
Reduce air pollution.
Recycle paper.
Save water.

WI 5: Families working together

Musical instruments

WI 6: Schools around the world

School related words
high school
middle school
a project
a uniform

WI 7: Lifestyles

Animals

Chunks
a shooting star
Let your heart decide.
Listen to your heart.
Take your time.

WI 8: Me & other animals

Chunks & nouns
animal caring / testing / training
fight against
live in harmony
organ transplants
vaccines

>>

Verb list

adopt (children)
be (I'm Clara. He's 13. They're from Chile.)
believe
borrow (a pencil, a book)
call (me Bob)
change (a person, the world)
chat (on MSN, online)
check (our schedule, the correct answer)
clean (the dormitory, the kitchen)
climb (trees, a mountain)
close (the door, your eyes, your book)
collect (comic books, soft toys)
come (here, in, on)
cook (lunch, dinner)
discover (important things)
divorce (from somebody)
do (your homework)
donate (money)
eat (cat food, insects, meat)
find (my MP4 player, your wallet)
fly (a kite, an airplane)
forget (it, your books)
get (home, in touch, my cell phone, real, up)
give (interviews, a present)
give up (doing something)
go (back to school, out, surfing, to bed)
hang out (with friends)
hate (math, traffic jams, cold days)
have (a car, breakfast, classes, fun, lots of problems, two sisters, blue eyes, fur)
help (a wild animal organization, Mom and Dad)
kill (animals)
know (you, my friend)
learn (about new things, two languages)
like (it, ice cream, science, tennis, playing soccer)
listen to (me, people, a CD, music)
live (with my family, next to the beach, in Orlando)
look (at me, at the board)
love (history, all sports, dancing, my city)
make (my bed, sense, a decision)
marry (somebody)
meet (me, my friend, my family)
miss (you all, your friend, your mom)
open (the book, your heart)
play (tennis, basketball, the guitar, the piano)
protect (people, animals, nature)
read (books, magazines, the horoscope pages)
remember (something, somebody)
ring (the bell)
save (water, yourself)
say (in English)
see (our schedule, you)
show (pictures)
sing (songs)
sit (down, side by side)
sleep (late)
spell (your name, a word)
stay (at school, at home)
stop (bullying, it)
study (at school, at home, English, French)
talk (about trips, in class, to your friends)
teach (surfing, English)
tell (the truth)
test (your friend)
think (about the animals, of a person)
train (your pet)
try (again, to love someone else)
turn on (the computer)
use (the wastebasket)
wake up (at 7 a.m.)
walk (to school, together)
want (to make a difference, to defend nature)
watch (TV)
work (for a TV series, hard)
write (e-mails, soon, your name, a message)

Track list

TRACK	PAGE	CONTENT
01	00	Introduction
02	04	Welcome Unit – L 1 – Ex.1
03	04	Welcome Unit – L 1 – Ex. 2
04	04	Welcome Unit – L 1 – Tip box
05	05	Welcome Unit – L 1 – Ex. 5
06	07	Welcome Unit – L 2 – Ex. 6
07	08	U 1 – L 1 – Ex. 1
08	10	U 1 – L 2 – Ex. 2
09	13	U 1 – L 3 – Ex. 4
10	14	U 1 – L 4 – Ex. 1
11	14	U 1 – L 4 – Ex. 3
12	18	U 2 – L 1 – Ex. 2
13	21	U 2 – L 2 – Ex. 3
14	23	U 2 – L 3 – Ex. 3
15	24	U 2 – L 4 – Ex. 1
16	28	U 3 – L 1 – Ex. 1
17	29	U 3 – L 1 – Ex. 4
18	30	U 3 – L 2 – Ex. 2
19	32	U 3 – L 3 – Ex. 1
20	34	U 3 – L 4 – Ex. 1
21	38	U 4 – L 1 – Ex. 1
22	40	U 4 – L 2 – Ex. 2
23	42	U 4 – L 3 – Ex. 1
24	44	U 4 – L 4 – Ex. 1
25	47	Review Lesson – Ex. 3
26	48	U 5 – L 1 – Ex. 1
27	50	U 5 – L 2 – Ex. 2
28	52	U 5 – L 3 – Ex. 1
29	54	U 5 – L 4 – Ex. 2
30	58	U 6 – L 1 – Ex. 1
31	60	U 6 – L 2 – Ex. 1
32	63	U 6 – L 3 – Ex. 5
33	64	U 6 – L 4 – Ex. 2
34	68	U 7 – L 1 – Ex. 1
35	70	U 7 – L 2 – Ex. 2
36	72	U 7 – L 3 – Ex. 1
37	78	U 8 – L 1 – Ex. 1
38	80	U 8 – L 2 – Ex. 1
39	82	U 8 – L 3 – Ex. 2
40	84	U 8 – L 4 – Ex. 2

Name **Class** **Date**

1 **Complete the table.**

Countries	Nationalities
Brazil	____________
____________	Venezuelan
____________	German
Great Britain	____________

2 **Find the countries and copy the words. Write the corresponding nationalities.**

TREYTHEUSAHJGUAETSOUTHAFRICAKGEAFECANADAKJARGENTINALAEXITALYJKGREECEJAFMEXICON

1 *The USA* *American*
2 ____________ ____________
3 ____________ ____________
4 ____________ ____________
5 ____________ ____________
6 ____________ ____________
7 ____________ ____________

3 **Complete the dialogue.**

Alice [1] ____________
Maria My name's Maria.
Alice And [2] ____________
Maria Maria Soares.
Alice [3] ____________
Maria I'm 11.
Alice I'm 11 too! [4] ____________
Maria I'm from Brazil.
Alice Nice to meet you!
Maria Nice to meet you too. Bye!

4 **There are FOUR mistakes in the text below. Rewrite the sentences correcting them.**

Hello. I'm Francesco. My last name is Francesco Gasparini.
I'm from italian. I 12 years old.

Hello. I'm Francesco. My full name is ____________

____

____

1 **Look at the flags and complete the sentences with *he* or *she*.**

1 ________'s from Japan.
2 ________'s from Colombia.
3 ________'s Brazilian.
4 ________'s from France.
5 ________'s Greek.

2 **This is John. Ask questions about him.**

1 ______________________________? He's from the USA.
2 ______________________________? 16? 17? I don't know!

3 **Hannah and Susan are at school. Complete their dialogue with *am ('m)*, *is ('s)* or *are ('re)*.**

Hannah Hey, Susan! I' [1] ______ in class 3B.
Susan Me too! That' [2] ______ great!
Hannah Look! This [3] ______ my friend Pilar.
Susan Where' [4] ______ she from?
Hannah She' [5] ______ from Bolivia.
Susan How old [6] ______ she?
Hannah She' [7] ______ 11. What about you?
You' [8] ______ 11 too, I think.
Susan No, wrong!
Hannah How old [9] ______ you, Susan?
Susan I' [10] ______ 12.
Hannah Me too!

4 **Write THREE sentences using the words from the box.**

she	he	you	is	am	are	old
Greece	from	12	I	how	Greek	Where

1 ______________________________
2 ______________________________
3 ______________________________

Name **Class** **Date**

1 Mix the colors. What do you get?

1 red + blue = purple
2 black + white = ______
3 yellow + red = ______
4 yellow + blue = ______
5 white + red = ______

2 Write the colors that you see in this picture.

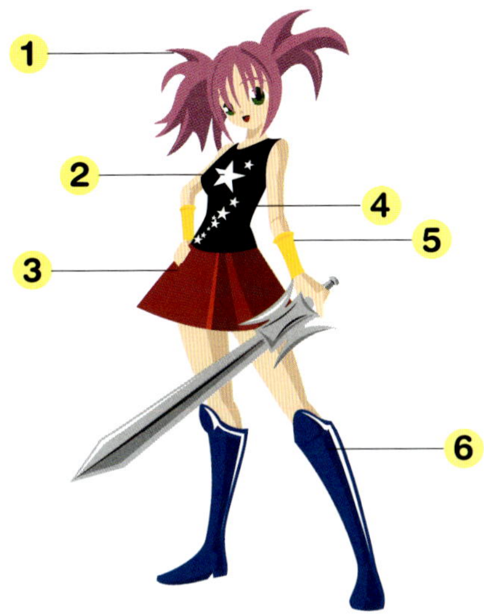

1 ______
2 ______
3 ______
4 ______
5 ______
6 ______

3 Check if **YOU** can answer these questions. Give short answers.

1 Is the South African flag black, purple and green? No, it isn't.
2 Is Brad Pitt French? No, ______
3 Is the American flag red, white and blue? Yes, ______
4 Is Jennifer Lopez American? Yes, ______
5 Is Mary-Kate Olsen German? No, ______
6 Are you from Brazil? ______

4 Unscramble the words to form questions.

1 is / Chinese / blue / the / and / flag / white
Is the ______? No, it isn't.
2 British / Madonna / is
______? No, she isn't.
3 Aaron Carter / is / American
______? Yes, he is.
4 is / flag / white / Brazilian / blue / the / yellow / and / green
______? Yes, it is.
5 Dennis / are / and / Francis / the USA / from
______? Yes, they are.

1 **Find SEVEN more months of the year in the wordsearch. Then write them.**

1 May
2 ______
3 ______
4 ______
5 ______
6 ______
7 ______
8 ______

Which is **YOUR** favorite month?

______

S	E	P	T	E	M	B	E	R	J	D	K
A	B	C	D	E	U	V	X	Y	Z	E	L
M	N	O	P	Q	R	J	C	D	E	C	Y
G	H	I	V	M	X	U	Y	Z	F	E	R
A	B	C	D	E	A	L	K	L	G	M	A
J	U	N	E	S	E	Y	C	B	F	B	U
D	C	B	N	A	F	G	H	I	G	E	N
D	H	A	U	G	U	S	T	F	H	R	A
L	I	R	P	A	Q	A	C	T	I	S	J

2 **Research. When are these holidays in the USA?**

1 Mother's Day is in ______.
2 Valentine's Day is in ______.
3 Father's Day is in ______.
4 Independence Day is in ______.

May | February | July | June

3 **Andy and Rita are new at school. Connect the words in the maze. Make SIX questions to complete their dialogue.**

Andy Hello. [1] What's your name?
Rita My name's Rita.
Andy [2] ______
Rita I'm 13 years old.
Andy [3] ______
Rita It's in February.
Andy [4] ______
Rita I'm from Brazil.
Andy [5] ______
Rita Well, my favorite color's green.
Andy [6] ______
Rita It's rb@adelphez.net.
Andy Thank you!

What's	How	old		
your	name?	are	you?	
Where	are	When's	your	address?
What's	you	What's	birthday?	e-mail
your	from?	your	What's	your
e-mail	address?	favorite	color?	

Name Class Date

1 Complete the crossword with parts of the body.

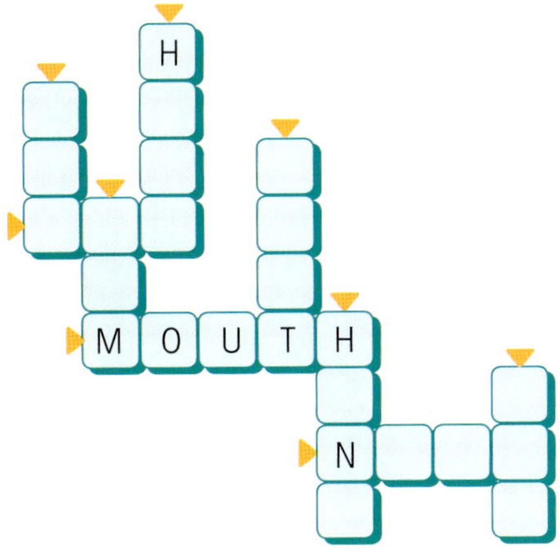

2 Add words to each group.

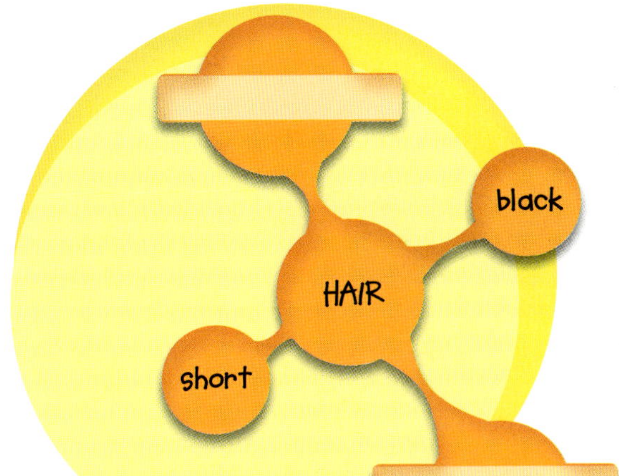

3 Use words from #1 and #2 to make FOUR sentences.

Example: My hair is brown and my eyes are brown too.

1 ____________________

2 ____________________

3 ____________________

4 ____________________

4 Read about Chris. Complete the column with information about **YOU**. Then complete the paragraph.

		YOU
Name	Chris	
Nationality	American	
Age	17	
Physical characteristics	short and strong black hair / blue eyes	
Personality	intelligent	

My name isn't Chris. My name's [1] ____________. I'm not American. I'm [2] ____________.
I'm not 17 years old. I [3] ____________.
[4] ____________ short and strong.
My hair [5] ____________ black and my eyes [6] ____________ blue. [7] ____________ intelligent.

1 **Which sport is it? Put the letters in the correct order and write the words.**

GRIUNSF
surfing

NCCLIGY
____

ESAKTANGOBRDI
____

GNSMWIM
____

What's YOUR favorite sport? Write a sentence.

____

2 **Complete the dialogue with the verb *to be*.**

Lea Hi, Chris. How [1] __________ you?

Chris I [2] __________ fine, thanks, Lea. Look at that new student. He [3] __________ from Colombia.

Lea [4] __________ he in class 2C?

Chris No, he [5] __________ . He [6] __________ in my class. We [7] __________ classmates.

Lea [8] __________ Mark and Sarah in your class too?

Chris No, they [9] __________ . They [10] __________ in class 3C.

3 **Unscramble the words to write questions. Then answer the questions.**

1 tennis player / you / Are / a / ?

Q Are you a tennis player?

A Yes, I am.

2 gymnast / Is / Diego Hipólito / a / ?

Q ____________________________

A Yes, ________________________

3 they / Are / surfers / ?

Q ____________________________

A No, ________________________

1 **Who is who? Look at the picture and read about these friends. Write the correct names.**

David is tall and strong. His hair is brown and his eyes are green. **Harry** is tall and slim. His hair is red and his eyes are green. **Jessica** is short and slim. Her hair is black. Her eyes are brown. **Sophie** is tall and slim. Her hair isn't short. It's brown and her eyes are brown too.

[1] ______________ [3] ______________

[2] ______________ [4] ______________

2 **Write *his* or *her*.**

1 Mark is tall. __________ hair is brown.

2 David's eyes are green and __________ hair is brown.

3 Jessica is in class 2C. __________ hair is black.

4 Sophie's tall. __________ eyes are brown.

3 **Complete the sentences using *he, his, she* or *her* according to the pictures.**

Susan

Daniel

1 __________ name is Susan.

2 __________ name's Daniel.

3 __________ hair is short.

4 __________ hair is dark brown.

5 __________ is from Canada.

6 __________ is American.

4 **Read about Hiroshi. Find FIVE mistakes in his profile. Underline and correct them.**

Hi! I'm Hiroshi. I'm 10 year old. I is Japanese. My favorite sport is tennis and my favorite tennis player are Roger Federer. My best friend is Gus. Her favorite sport is swimming.

1 __________

2 __________

3 __________

4 __________

1 Circle the correct option to complete the sentences.

1 This is Mark. **His / Her** favorite band is Infected Mushrooms.
2 Look at Emma. **His / Her** hair is short and black.
3 These are Henry and Joe. **Our / Their** favorite sport is soccer.
4 We're classmates. **Our / Their** class is 2B.
5 Who's **their / your** favorite teacher? My favorite teacher is Miss Harris.

2 Underline the word that doesn't belong in the group.

1 cycling – swimming – athlete – tennis
2 awesome – rude – gorgeous – charming
3 our – their – my – we

3 Give YOUR opinion about the people below.

1 Gisele Bündchen I think she's beautiful and intelligent.
2 Jennifer Lopez ______
3 Johnny Depp ______
4 Gustavo Kuerten ______

4 Chris and Vera are e-pals. Complete Chris's e-mail with the phrases from the box.

How are you? | Write soon! Bye! | Dear Vera, | he's very intelligent and funny

My New School

To: veraV778@dial.com
From: chris435@dial.com
Subject: My new teacher

new e-mail | reply | forward

[1] ______
Hi! [2] ______ We have a new English teacher at school.
His name's is Mr. Taylor.
I think he's fantastic: [3] ______. He's tall and slim. His hair is brown and his eyes are green.

[4] ______

Chris

Name **Class** **Date**

1 **Look at the pictures. Complete the sentences using *this* or *that*.**

1 ________ is a book.

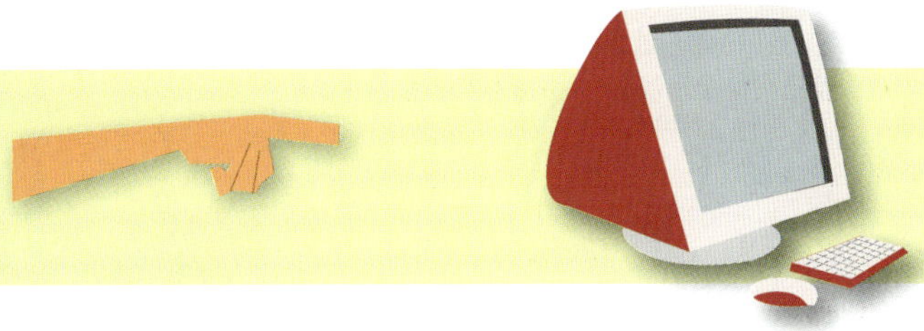

2 ________ is a computer.

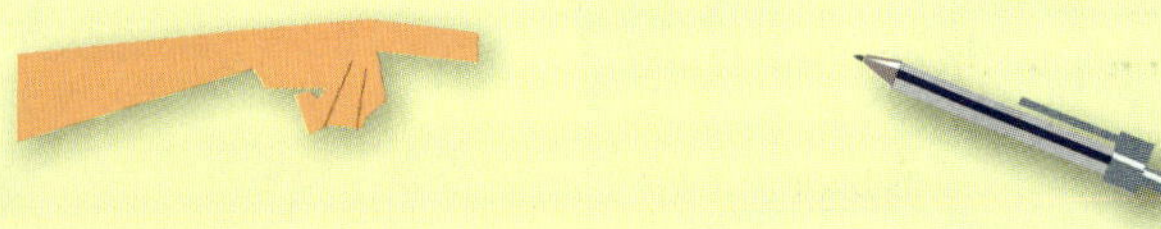

3 ________ is a pen.

2 **Find NINE classroom objects. Write them in the list using *a* or *an*.**

Classroom Objects

1 a whiteboard
2 ________
3 ________
4 ________
5 ________
6 ________
7 ________
8 ________
9 ________

LEWHITEBOARDDESKRNIPENCILCASEANOTEBOOKGRCOMPUTERERASER

3 **Write THREE sentences about YOUR classroom objects.**

1 ________________________________
2 ________________________________
3 ________________________________

1 **Look at the pictures. Complete the speech bubbles with *these* or *those*.**

2 **Sally and Gabriel are friends. Write sentences about their belongings. Follow the model.**

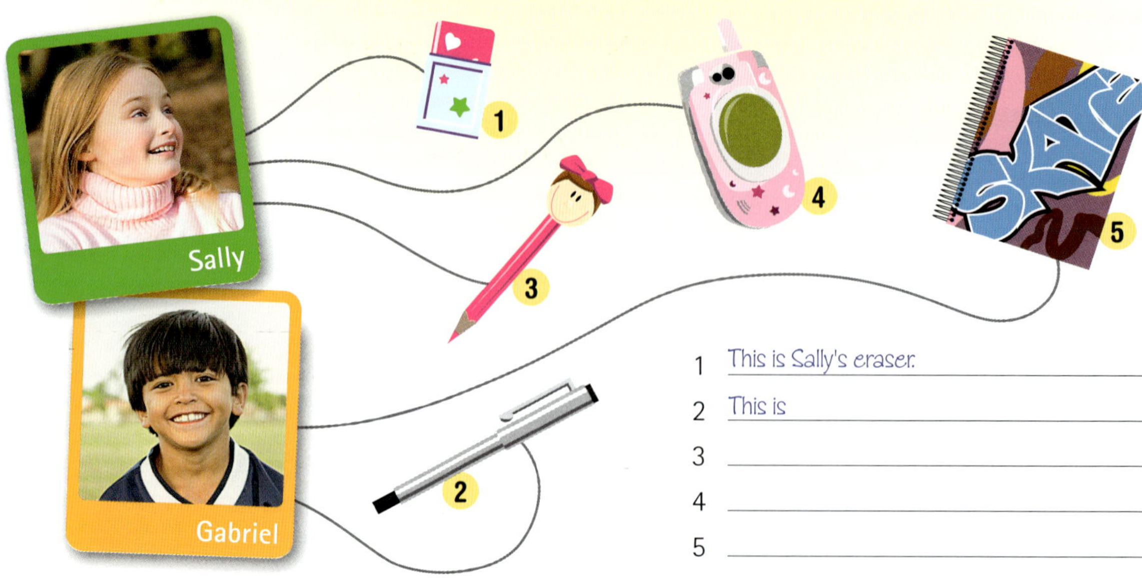

1 This is Sally's eraser.

2 This is ______

3 ______

4 ______

5 ______

Name **Class** **Date**

1 **Complete using the words in the box.**

that	these	this	those	Nancy's

2 **Check (✓) the correct option to complete the dialogues.**

1 *Mary* Let's play a computer game.
Joan ◯ That's a good idea! ◯ It's Martha's computer.

2 *Mary* Let's watch TV.
Joan ◯ What are those? ◯ Oh no. Let's do something else!

3 *Mary* What are those?
Joan ◯ It's my pen. ◯ They're my pens.

3 **Now YOU write sentences. Use these words.**

that's	roller skates	her	MP4 player	glasses	my
Lucy's	those	those	his		
they're	are	umbrella	Matchbox cars	is	
cell phone	is	a	Peter's	this	are

That's a cell phone.

___

___

___

___

Unit 3 - lesson 3 Workbook

1 **Complete with *and* or *but*.**

1 Sean Lennon is American, ________ his mother is from Japan.
2 Tanaka is Japanese ________ her favorite sport is baseball.
3 Lin's favorite singers are Hilary Duff ________ Jesse McCartney.
4 Maurice is from Spain, ________ his favorite athlete isn't Spanish.
5 Lara's favorite sport is volleyball ________ she is on the school team.

2 **Connect words in the maze and write THREE sentences.**
Example: *Bob's favorite sport is soccer.*

1 Maria is ____
2 Pierre ____
3 ____

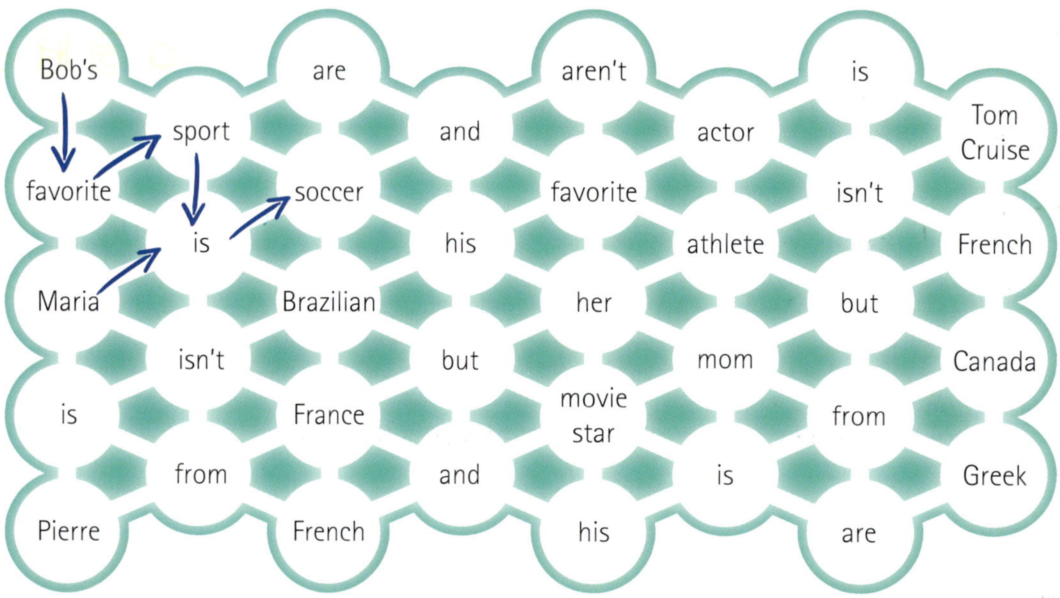

Can you write a different sentence using these words?

____

3 **Read the information about Juan. Then finish writing a paragraph about him.**

Name	Juan
Nationality	Chilean
Parents' nationality	Brazilian
Favorite sport	soccer
Favorite band	Black Eyed Peas
Favorite actor	Will Smith
Favorite athlete	Ronaldinho Gaúcho

Juan is from Chile, but his parents ....

Name Class Date

1 **Underline the word that doesn't belong in each group.**

1 the principal – students – a gym – teachers
2 a cafeteria – a supermarket – a computer lab – an auditorium
3 music – soccer – basketball – football – ice skating
4 foreign language – drama – music – hockey

Choose one word and write a sentence.

____

2 **Write the words under the correct column.**

classrooms – auditorium – computer lab – gym – posters – health office – students – cafeteria – glasses

a	an	∅
		classrooms

3 **This is the floor plan for Santa Fe Middle School. Use the plan to write sentences about the school. Use *there is* and *there are*.**

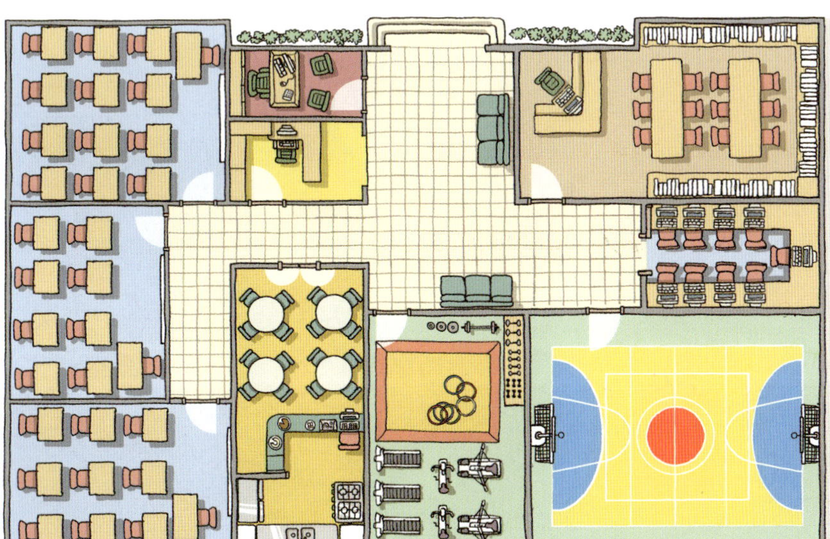

On the first floor of Santa Fe Middle School [1] ________ a computer lab. [2] ________ two gyms, [3] ________ a cafeteria and the principal's office too. [4] ________ a library and [5] ________ three classrooms. It's a nice school!

Unit 4 - lesson 1

Workbook

1 **Write the names of the objects and find the secret word.**

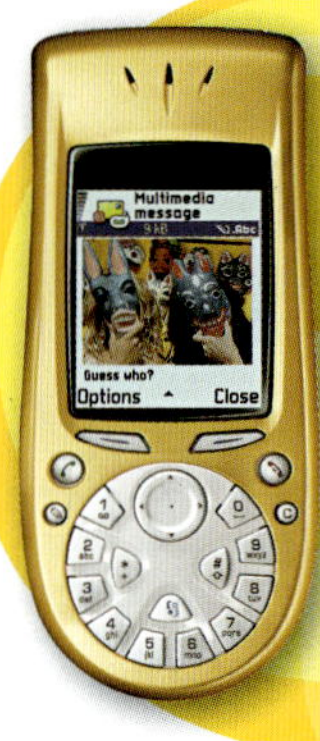

C E L L P H O N E

U M B R E L L A

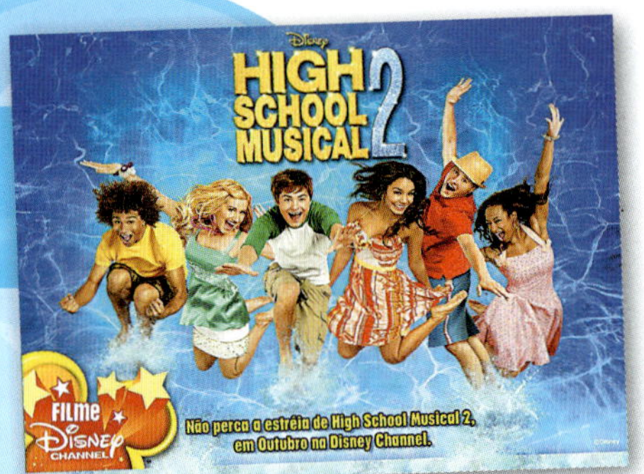

P O E S T E R

The secret word is:

C O M P U T E R

Is there a computer in *YOUR* bedroom? Where is it?

____

2 **Complete the questions with *Where is* or *Where are*. Then look at the picture and answer the questions.**

1 Where's the computer?
It's on the desk.

2 Where are the pencils?
They're in the bag

3 Where's the backpack?
It's on the computer

4 Where are the glasses?
They're behind the books

5 Where are the books?
They're in front of the glasses

6 Where's the wallet?
It's next to the books

Name **Class** **Date**

1 **Check (✓) the correct questions to complete the dialogue.**

Rita Hi, Muriel. So, what do you think of your new neighborhood?

Muriel I love it! It's great!

Rita ◯ Is there a mall near your house?
◯ There is a mall near your house?

Muriel Yes! And there is a cybercafé too!

Rita ◯ Cool! Is there any supermarkets?
◯ Cool! Are there any supermarkets?

Muriel There's one near here. It's really big!

Rita ◯ Are there a restaurant?
◯ Are there any restaurants?

Muriel Yes, there are three or four, I think. Italian, Chinese, Mexican...

Rita ◯ That's fantastic! Is there a subway station?
◯ That's fantastic! Are there a subway station?

Muriel No, there isn't. What about paying me a visit?

Rita Great idea!

2 **Peter lives in an area of houses and farms only. Change the sentences to the negative form to make true sentences about his neighborhood.**

1 There is a hospital.
There isn't a hospital. / There is no hospital.

2 There are stores.

3 There is a park.

4 There is a mall.

1 **What's the result? Write in full.**

1 eleven + twelve + twenty – thirteen + two – ten + five = ____________________

2 twenty-five – twenty + five + twenty = ____________________

3 forty-eight – thirty-one – six + thirty-nine = ____________________

4 fifty – twenty-seven + twelve – eleven + thirty-one = ____________________

2 **Look at the picture. Ask questions with *How many* and answer them.**

1 How many pens are there? There are ____________________

2 __________ books __________ There are ____________________

3 ____________________ There are thirteen ____________________

4 ____________________ There are three ____________________

5 ____________________ There are __________ cell phones.

6 __________ balls __________ There are ____________________

3 **PUZZLE: what's the secret sentence?**
Solve the problems. Write the results. Change each result into its corresponding letter. Find the secret sentence.

25 = A 36 = E 48 = G 4 = O 42 = R 50 = T 12 = U 30 = Y

10 x 3 = 30 ➡ Y
2 x 2 = ______ ➡ ______
3 x 4 = ______ ➡ ______

5 x 5 = 25 ➡ A
6 x 7 = ______ ➡ ______
6 x 6 = ______ ➡ ______

6 x 8 = 48 ➡ G
25 + 17 = ______ ➡ ______
52 – 16 = ______ ➡ ______
100 ÷ 5 = ______ ➡ ______
5 x 10 = ______ ➡ ______

The secret sentence is: Y______ A______ G________!

Name **Class** **Date**

1 **Look at Michael's family and then unscramble the words to say who each person is.**

1 Lucy is Michael's ______________________ (nmheaogtrdr)
2 Peter is Michael's ______________________ (hteefrtsap)
3 Sharon is Michael's ______________________ (hemrot)
4 Kassandra is Michael's ______________________ (tsries alhf)
5 Paul is Michael's ______________________ (Incue)
6 Dorothy is Michael's ______________________ (tnau)

2 **Look at the sentences in #1. Complete the sentences below with the correct names.**

1 Michael is ______________ son.
2 Michael is ______________ stepson.
3 Michael is ______________ half brother.

3 **Rewrite the sentences using *is* whenever possible.**

1 My father's name's Samuel. *My father's name is Samuel.*
2 That's my grandmother's house. ______________________
3 Olivia's cell phone's blue. ______________________
4 My aunt's married to my teacher's brother. ______________________

4 **Check (✓) the grammatically correct sentences. Make corrections whenever necessary.**

1 ◯ My mother' parents are divorced. *My mother's parents are divorced.*
2 ◯ I love my grandparents'. ______________________
3 ◯ My mother's name's Jane. ______________________
4 ◯ That's my cousins house. Their house is big. ______________________
5 ◯ James's brother is in class 3B. ______________________

1 **Write in the parts of the body.**

1 hair
2 ______
3 ______
4 ______
5 ______
6 ______
7 ______
8 ______
9 hand
10 ______
11 ______
12 ______
13 ______

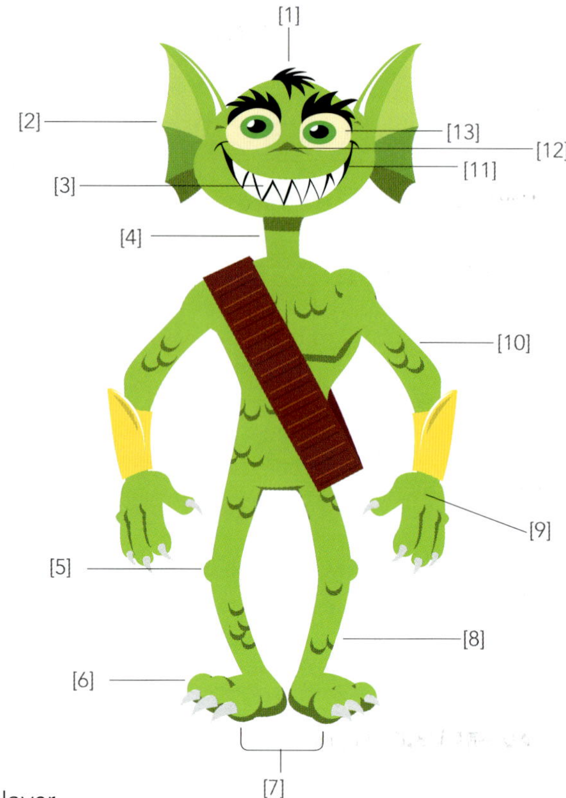

2 **Circle the correct answer.**

1 Lynne **have / has** a pink cell phone and a brown MP4 player.
2 I **have / has** two brothers and my friend, Wayne, **have / has** three sisters.
3 My uncle and aunt **have / has** a big house in New Jersey.
4 My sister and I **have / has** a big bedroom.
5 Our children **have / has** lots of friends.
6 Mary **have / has** long legs.

3 **Complete the description with *is* or *has*.**

My favorite movie star [1] ______ Orlando Bloom. He [2] ______ from Britain and he [3] ______ about 30 years old. He [4] ______ a sister, Samantha. Orlando [5] ______ brown hair and beautiful brown eyes. I think he [6] ______ a very good actor.

4 **Unscramble the words to make sentences.**

1 sister / my / beautiful / hair / has / .

______

2 long / giraffes / have / necks / and / ears / funny / .

______

3 has / green / Shrek / skin / fat / a / and / body / .

______

Name **Class** **Date**

1 Match the sports and the pictures.

[ ] tennis
[ ] volleyball
[ ] cycling
[ ] surfing
[ ] hang gliding
[ ] skateboarding

1

2

3

4

5

6

2 Choose YOUR favorite sport from the list in #1 and write a sentence.

____
____
____

3 Choose words and expressions below.

Let's
What about...?

+

surfing / watching a DVD / going to a museum / have a party / playing in the park / go surfing / watch a DVD / go bowling / a party / bowling / go to a museum / play in the park

Which suggestions would YOU make...

1 to your English teacher? ______________________________
2 to your best friend? ______________________________
3 to your mother or father? ______________________________
4 to a classmate? ______________________________

4 Complete the dialogue with the words from the box.

a movie about going good
great have idea know surf
surfing watch way

Anne Let's go [1] ______________ .
Dad [2] ______________ idea!
Paul No [3] ______________ ! I hate sports!
Mom Well, what about [4] ______________ ?
Anne I don't [5] ______________ . It's such a beautiful day! Perfect for surfing!
Paul I have an idea, Anne. Mom and I [6] ______________ a movie and you and Dad go surfing.
Anne [7] ______________ !

1 **Look at the occupations below. Write THREE sentences about the people in YOUR family.**

doctor sales clerk police officer farmer teacher web designer architect tour guide flight attendant manager

Example: My uncle isn't a manager.

1 ______________________________

2 ______________________________

3 ______________________________

2 **Check (✓) the correct options.**

1 ◯ **There is** ◯ **Has** a doctor in my building. He's my neighbor.
2 ◯ **There is** ◯ **Has** a flight attendant in my family.
3 My best friend ◯ **there is** ◯ **has** a gym at his home.
4 ◯ **Have** ◯ **There are** many architects in my family.
5 ◯ **There are** ◯ **Have** farmers in Danny's neighborhood.

3 **Read the paragraph about Oscar. Underline FIVE grammar or vocabulary mistakes. Correct them.**

My name's Oscar and I'm from Quito, the capital city of Ecuador. I live in a big house with my fathers, Diego and Tatiana. I has two brothers and a sister. My brothers's names are Alejandro and Javier and my sister's name is Bianca. My grandfather and my grandmother are farmers. Their names is David and Pilar. My father has one brother. His name's Fernando. My mother has two brothers and a sister, but Fernando's my favorite aunt!

1 parents ________ 2 ________ 3 ________ 4 ________ 5 ________

4 **Read the paragraph again. Write T for *true* and F for *false*.**

1 [ ] Oscar is from Ecuador.
2 [ ] His father's name is Alejandro.
3 [ ] Javier is Oscar's brother and Pilar is Oscar's grandmother.
4 [ ] Oscar has no aunts.

Name Class Date

1 Find SIX school subjects. What's **YOUR** favorite? ____________

When do you have it at school? ____________

1 English
2 ____________
3 ____________
4 ____________
5 ____________
6 ____________

E	N	G	L	I	S	H	A	G	S
V	M	E	U	A	C	T	T	U	G
I	C	O	J	D	I	A	R	T	S
E	S	G	G	H	E	M	A	R	I
H	I	R	B	I	N	D	E	O	Y
N	O	A	J	S	C	G	I	P	T
K	E	P	I	G	E	J	C	B	H
G	R	H	E	L	C	B	M	O	R
Y	F	Y	R	O	T	S	I	H	T

2 Complete the table about **YOU**.

	School subjects	Singers	Movie stars
I like			
I don't like			
I love			
I hate			

3 Write sentences using the words from #1 and 2. Use *but* in all sentences.

1 I like ____________ , but I don't like ____________ .
2 I hate ____________ , but I love ____________ .
3 ____________ .
4 ____________ .

4 Give **YOUR** opinion. Write sentences using *I like*, *I don't like*, *I love* or *I hate*.

Example:  I like basketball.

1  ____________

2  ____________

3  ____________

4  ____________

1 **Pedro is Brazilian. He's from Brasília and studies in an American school. Read his schedule. What is he saying? Complete the sentences.**

	MON	TUE	WED	THU	FRI
a.m.	math	science	math	geography	English
p.m.	history	PE	Portuguese	art	art

I have science on Tuesday mornings.
I have math ______________________.
______________ on Tuesday afternoons.
______________ Portuguese on ______________ afternoons.
I have ______________ on Thursday ______________.
I have art ______________________.

2 **Fill in the blanks with *I have* or *I don't have* to make true sentences about YOU.**

1 ______________________ home economics at school.
2 ______________________ computer lessons.
3 ______________________ classes on Saturdays.
4 ______________________ music lessons at school.

3 **Create YOUR ideal schedule.**

	MON	TUE	WED	THU	FRI
A.M.					
P.M.					

Name Class Date

1 What time is it? Look at the clocks and write the times.

1 8:15 It's eight fifteen. ______

2 11:00 It's ______

3 5:45 ______

4 12:00 P.M. ______

5 7:20 ______

6 12:00 A.M. ______

2 Sally's a busy girl. Read about her routine and do the exercises.

We have math at eight o'clock on Mondays. I love math! We have English on Wednesdays and art on Tuesdays and Thursdays at four o'clock. PE class is on Mondays at three-thirty. I hate PE! We have science on Tuesdays and Fridays and on Wednesdays we have geography at nine fifteen. My history class is on Thursdays. I do my homework every day from five thirty to six. My bed time is at ten and I have a shower before I go to bed.

Complete her school schedule.

	MON	TUE	WED	THU	FRI
a.m.	math 8:00	science 10:30		8:00	science 10:30
p.m.			English 2:10		Free

Answer the questions.

1 When is Sally's homework time? ______

2 When is her bath time? ______

3 When is her bed time? ______

3 Read the notes. Complete the sentences using *in*, *on*, *at* or *from – to*.

Pet shop
open
10:00 a.m. →
5:00 p.m.

Saturday
Tennis class

Sunday
afternoons
Play soccer

evenings
Watch TV

1 The pet shop is open ______ 10:00 a.m. ______ 5:00 p.m.

2 I have tennis classes ______ Saturdays ______ 9:00 a.m.

3 I play soccer ______ Sunday afternoons.

4 I watch TV ______ the evenings.

1 Read the sentences. Check (✓) the correct option.

1 A Where's the teacher?
B She's ______ the first floor.
◯ in ◯ on ◯ from

2 Let's have a party ______ our classroom.
◯ at ◯ on ◯ in

3 A Where's Dad?
B He's ______ work.
◯ on ◯ at ◯ in

4 A When is our English test?
B It's ______ Monday.
◯ on ◯ at ◯ in

2 Find and underline SIX mistakes. Correct them.

My favorite day at school is Monday. I like PE on Mondays and I love it. My PE teacher is Mr. Johnson. She's tall and her hair is blond. My PE class is on 10:30 at the 2nd floor. I have classes on the library on Mondays too. It's a great day!

1 have 2 ______ 3 ______ 4 ______ 5 ______ 6 ______

3 Use the prompts to write questions. Add any necessary words. Then answer the questions about **YOU**.

1 bullies / your / school / ?
Q Are there bullies at your school?
A ______

2 when / your / bath time / ?
Q ______
A ______

3 your classroom / second floor / ?
Q ______
A ______

4 many / boys / class / ?
Q ______
A ______

Name Class Date

1 **Match the columns.**

1 do
2 play
3 have
4 go
5 get
6 watch
7 take
8 brush

[3] breakfast
[ ] to school
[ ] home
[ ] soccer
[ ] dressed
[ ] up
[ ] your teeth
[ ] to bed
[ ] TV
[ ] (my) homework
[3] lunch
[ ] tennis
[ ] dinner
[ ] a shower

2 **Match EIGHT activities in #1 to the pictures below.**

1 get up

2 ____________

3 ____________

4 ____________

5 ____________

6 ____________

7 ____________

8 ____________

3 **Now write about YOUR routine. Use the activities from #1.**

I get up at ____________

1 **Jason is at a summer camp. Read his e-mail to his parents. Use the illustrations to write the missing activities.**

Summer camp!

To: john198N@dial.com
From: jason692@dial.com
Subject: Summer camp!

new e-mail | reply | forward

Hi, everybody!

The summer camp is great! I love it! First thing in the mornings,

I  [1] ______________________. It's boring, but it's OK! We have breakfast and then we  [2] ______________________ or we  [3] ______________________ in the lake. After lunch, we  [4] ______________________ and  [5] ______________________.

It's really fun! I love it!
See you soon!

Jason

2 **Check (✓) the correct verb to complete the sentences.**

1 My friends and I ◯ **cook** / ◯ **go** dinner together.

2 We ◯ **make** / ◯ **go** sailing in the afternoons.

3 Every morning I ◯ **make** / ◯ **go** my bed.

4 In the evenings we ◯ **go** / ◯ **play** computer games.

5 We ◯ **play** / ◯ **have** arts & crafts classes too.

3 **Choose THREE sentences from #2 and write a paragraph. Use *first*, *then* and *after that* to connect the sentences.**

____

____

____

____

Name **Class** **Date**

1 **Justin and Mike are brothers. This table shows how they go to different places. Look at the table and answer the questions.**

	school	mall	sports club	grandmother's house
	✓			
				✓
		✓		
			✓	

1 How do they go to the mall?
By subway. / They go to the mall by subway.

2 How do they go to their grandmother's house?
____

3 How do they go to the sports club?
____

4 How do they go to school?
____

2 **Add any necessary words to these ones to make questions.**

1 Q go / school / bike / ? Do you go to school by bike?
A Yes, I do. / No, I don't.

2 Q have breakfast / every morning / ? __________
A __________

3 Q get up / 7 a.m. / weekend / ? __________
A __________

4 Q have English / Thursdays / ? __________
A __________

5 Q take a shower / before school / ? __________
A __________

Now go back and give YOUR answers to the questions.

1 **Karina is Canadian. She has a popular blog on the Net. Use the information below to complete it.**

	KARINA	LUCY	LINDA
age	12	13	16
nationality	Canadian		
bedrooms	One bedroom for Karina and Lucy		One bedroom for Linda
collection	X		
free time activities		SPORTS = 	
pets			

February 25th | Create a blog | Login

Welcome to my blog!

My name's Karina. I'm 12 and I'm from [1] Canada.
I have two sisters, Lucy and [2] ______. They [3] ______ 13 and 16. We [4] ______ in a big house in a quiet neighborhood of Toronto. Lucy and I share a bedroom. In our room, Lucy and I [5] ______ books, talk and [6] ______ computer games. I [7] ______ a collection. Lucy collects [8] ______ and Linda collects [9] ______. Linda [10] ______ her own bedroom! She loves [11] ______ and she [12] ______ tennis too. Lucy and I [13] ______ sports! We have two pets: a cat and a [14] ______. Linda hates dogs so we [15] ______ a dog!

I love my family!

Search OK

Older posts ...

Links ...

2 **Unscramble the words to make sentences.**

1 don't / at / cousins / get up / my / 6 o'clock /.

______

2 play / my / don't / brothers / little / basketball / .

______

3 bed / make / my / don't / I / .

______

4 stickers / they / collect / don't / .

______

Name **Class** **Date**

1 **Caroline is an Australian teen. Complete the text about her. Use the verbs in the box in their correct form.**

be (3x)	love	think	go (2x)	live	play (2x)	have	study

Caroline [1] _______ from Australia. Every day she [2] _______ to school by bike. She [3] _______ very intelligent and she [4] _______ sports.
She [5] _______ tennis lessons on Mondays and Wednesdays and she [6] _______ volleyball on Tuesdays and Thursdays.
In the evenings she [7] _______ for school and on weekends she [8] _______ dancing and [9] _______ soccer on the beach.
Her boyfriend [10] _______ in New Zealand with his mom, dad and two brothers. She chats online with him every day. He [11] _______ a surfing teacher. He [12] _______ Caroline's fantastic!

2 **Read the text again. Check (✓) the correct option.**

1 Caroline and her boyfriend ◯ **chat** ◯ **chats** online every day.

2 Caroline ◯ **go** ◯ **goes** to the beach on Sundays.

3 Caroline's boyfriend and his family ◯ **live** ◯ **lives** in New Zealand.

3 **Look at the pictures. Write more about Caroline.**

1 Caroline ___loves___ dogs.
2 She _______ at 7 a.m. every day.
3 She _______ golf.
4 She _______ two brothers.

1 **Discover the mystery pet.**

1 Its fur is soft. It likes to play.
It eats fish.

2 It has red and blue feathers
and a black and white beak.

3 It's small and of different colors.
It lives in the water.

4 It has short legs and a long tail.
It eats insects.

5 It's quiet and interesting to watch.
It's sometimes dangerous.

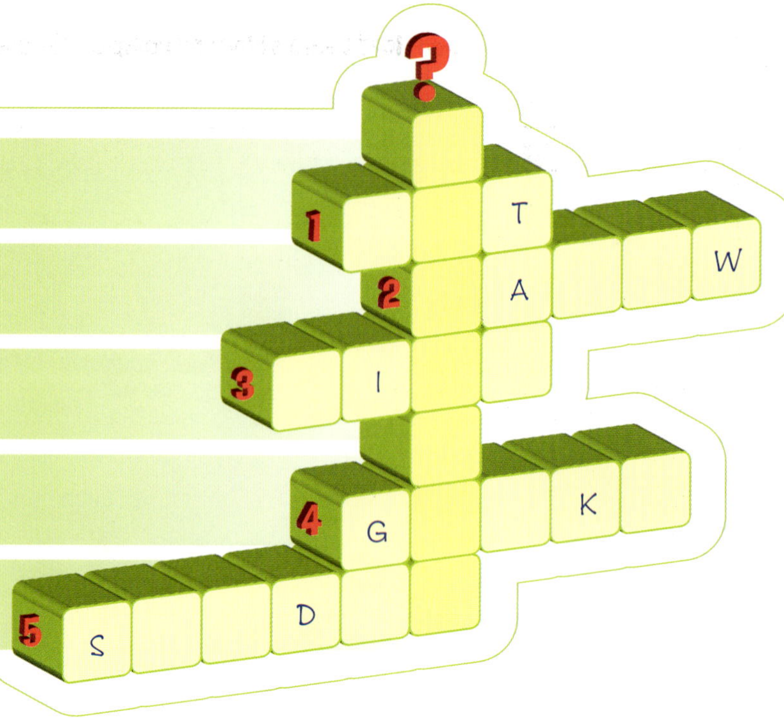

2 **Choose TWO other pets YOU like. Describe them. Look at the sentences in #1 for reference.**

1 Pet: ______________________
____
____

2 Pet: ______________________
____
____

3 **Go back to Karina's blog on page 132. Use the prompts below to ask and answer questions about her and her family.**

1 Karina / have / sisters / ?
Does Karina have sisters?
Yes, ______________________________

2 Karina / live / in New York / ?
____
____

3 her sister Lucy / collect / stickers / ?
____
____

4 Karina / have / a bird / ?
____
____

4 **Complete the table about YOUR real or imaginary pet. Write a paragraph.**

Pet ______________________

Name ______________________

Description: ....
....

Lives in: ....

Eats: ....

Likes: ....

Your opinion: ....
....

I have a ....
His / her name ....
....
....
....
....
....
....
....
....

1 **Laura is a teen who loves cats. Read Laura's blog and complete the sentences below in the affirmative or negative.**

Laura Woodward

Create a blog | Login

September 21st

Laura Woodward BLOG

search OK

older posts ...

links ...

WELCOME TO MY BLOG!

Are you a cat person, or a dog person?

Filed under: life, blogging, pets @ 3:05 p.m.

Tags: cat, dog, pet

I'm a cat person. I love them. Don't get me wrong: I don't hate dogs, but I think they are silly and messy. Tina, my cat, is fantastic: she sleeps during the day and is very active at night. She climbs up the doors and the fridge but she doesn't break anything. She's a real lady. There's a saying: "Dogs have owners, cats have staff." Tina is independent, but at the same time a great companion. So which are you? A cat person, or a dog person?

COMMENTS

I live with a group of dog people so that's what I am: a dog person by association. Tyra, my 2-year-old dog, is a real good friend. She doesn't bite. I take her for walks in the park and she's so obedient that I don't need to keep her on a leash. I think cats are distant and they don't care about people. I don't like them.

Comment by Peter Davidson - September 23rd @ 1:15 a.m.

1 Laura ______________________ (have) a cat.
2 She ______________________ (hate) dogs.
3 Tina ______________________ (sleep) at night.
4 Peter ______________________ (like) cats.
5 Peter ______________________ (keep) his dog on a leash.
6 Peter ______________________ (take) Tyra for walks.
7 Tyra ______________________ (bite).
8 Tyra ______________________ (disobey) Peter.

1 **Check (✓) the table about YOUR daily routine.**

	ALWAYS	OFTEN	SOMETIMES	NEVER
1 WHAT TIME DO YOU GET UP FROM MONDAY TO FRIDAY?				
At 7:00				
At 8:00				
At 9:00				
2 HOW DO YOU GO TO SCHOOL?				
By car				
By bus				
On foot				
3 WHAT DO YOU DO AFTER SCHOOL?				
Watch TV				
Play sports				
Do my homework				
4 WHAT DO YOU DO ON WEEKEND?				
Play computer games				
Go to the mall				
Eat out				

2 **Write sentences using the information from #1.**

Example: *I often get up at 6:00. I never get up at 9:00.*

1 ______________________________

2 ______________________________

3 ______________________________

4 ______________________________

3 **Write the adjectives in the positive / negative continuum.**

determined, angry, quiet, impatient, intelligent, patient, critical, popular, shy, practical, courageous, creative

(+) Positive		(-) Negative
courageous		

4 **Choose two adjectives to describe YOUR personality.**

I'm ____________________ and ____________________ .